国务院侨务办公室立项　彭磷基人才培养改革基金资助

西方文化与艺术鉴赏

An Introduction to Western Culture and Art

谢工曲 | 编著

·广州·

版权所有 翻印必究

图书在版编目（CIP）数据

西方文化与艺术鉴赏 / 谢工曲编著 . —广州：中山大学出版社，2018.8
ISBN 978-7-306-06425-7

Ⅰ.①西… Ⅱ.①谢… Ⅲ.①英语—阅读教学—高等学校—教材②艺术—鉴赏—西方国家 Ⅳ.① H319.37:J

中国版本图书馆 CIP 数据核字（2018）第 194792 号

XIFANG WENHUA YU YISHU JIANSHANG

出 版 人：	王天琪
策划编辑：	林彩云
责任编辑：	林彩云
封面设计：	曾 斌
责任校对：	刘学谦
责任技编：	何雅涛
出版发行：	中山大学出版社
电　　话：	编辑部 020-84111996，84113349，84111997，84110779
	发行部 020-84111998，84111981，84111160
地　　址：	广州市新港西路 135 号
邮　　编：	510275　　传　　真：020-84036565
网　　址：	http://www.zsup.com.cn　　E-mail：zdcbs@mail.sysu.edu.cn
印 刷 者：	广州家联印刷有限公司
规　　格：	787mm×1092mm　1/16　11 印张　230 千字
版次印次：	2018 年 8 月第 1 版　2018 年 8 月第 1 次印刷
定　　价：	58.00 元

如发现本书因印装质量影响阅读，请与出版社发行部联系调换

序　言

欧陆风情、东方威尼斯、托斯卡纳风格……每天，各种西方文化艺术元素和标志以不同形式进入我们的生活，并影响着我们。但是，这类文化艺术元素都代表了什么？它们是怎样形成的？它们之间有什么相互关联性？它们对我们的生活有什么影响和启示呢？

为了探究这些问题，2015年暑期，编者便沿着欧洲铁路线，寻访艺术大师的足迹，开启了源自17—19世纪欧洲青年崇尚的文化朝圣（可称之为"壮游"/Grand Tour）、"游学"欧洲博物馆之旅。本次文化艺术之旅的构想历经数年筛选凝练，编者现将其感悟集结成册，以飨读者。在此感谢编者的亲人、朋友和同事鼎力相助，使本书中各种艺术风格的图片资料更加丰富充实。

西方社会历经数千年的发展整合，其文化艺术既表现出一致性，又呈现出复杂性和多彩性。本书在对西方文化艺术进行探索的过程中，着重对它的起源、形成与发展、风貌特征进行概述，力求在较完整地展示西方文化艺术的内涵和发展历程的同时，更凸显贯穿其中推动西方文明进程和对人类社会进步产生深远影响的思想、运动和成就。

本书以西方社会发展演变的脉络为主线，图文并茂地描述人们的生活场景、城市形态、建筑与艺术风格的发展演变过程及其相互关联性，形成一个描述西方社会及文化艺术的动态影像。本书通过对西方文化艺术的纵向历史发展演变和横向不同观点的阐述分析，使读者初步掌握西方文化艺术的发展过程和纷繁复杂的种种表现，以此激发读者对西方文化艺术的本质与意义的思索。

本书包括古埃及文化、古希腊文化、古罗马文化、基督教文化、中世纪哥特文化、伊斯兰文化、拜占庭文化、文艺复兴、启蒙运动和现代主义等内容，涉及西方文化艺术史上有重大影响的文化发展时期和经济技术发展状况，勾勒出一个较为完整的西方文化艺术坐标体系，许多历史风格的形成与发展在很大程度上是应对时代发展需求的。

本书具有明确的针对性，对学生丰富跨文化体验、了解西方文化与艺术的发展进程很有帮助，可作为英语翻译、旅游、建筑设计、艺术设计、广告设计、包装设计、对外汉语教学等专业学科的专业选修课或公共选修课教材；同时也可为普通读者到欧洲旅游或了解西方文化与艺术提供参考与借鉴作用，为读者获取相关专业知识提供语言素材和专业的英语表达方式。

Contents

Chapter One The Ancient Egyptian Culture 1
  1.1 Geographical Environment 3
  1.2 Achievements in Art and Architecture 4
    1.2.1 The Development of Pyramid 4
    1.2.2 Temple 7
    1.2.3 Art 7

Chapter Two Ancient Greek Culture 12
  2.1 Geographical Environment 12
  2.2 Greek City-states 13
  2.3 The Achievements of Greek Culture 15
  2.4 The Achievements in Architecture and Art 17
    2.4.1 Classical Orders 17
    2.4.2 Temple 17
    2.4.3 Theatre 19
  2.5 Art and Sculpture 21
  2.6 The Fall of Greek Culture 23

Chapter Three Ancient Roman Culture 26
  3.1 Geographical Environment 26
  3.2 From Republic to Empire 29
  3.3 Roman Technological Achievements 32
  3.4 Art and Architecture 36

Chapter Four Early Christianity 43
  4.1 Church and Monasticism 46
    4.1.1 Early Christian Architecture and Art (100–500 AD) 46
    4.1.2 Introduction of Monasticism 51

Chapter Five The Early Middle Ages 53
  5.1 The Later Roman Empire 54
  5.2 The Middle Ages (500–1500 AD) 54
  5.3 The Early Middle Ages (500–1000 AD) 54
    Pilgrimage 58
  5.4 Romanesque Art and Architecture 60

Chapter Six Islamic Culture 66
  6.1 Muslim Conquest (632–750 AD) 66
  6.2 The Flourish of Islamic Culture 67
    6.2.1 Pilgrimage and Trade 69
    6.2.2 Urbanization 70
  6.3 Muslim Influence in Spain 70
  6.4. Moorish Art and Architecture 72

Chapter Seven Byzantine Culture 79
  7.1 Byzantine Empire (330–1453 AD) 79
  7.2 Byzantine Architecture and Art 80

  7.3 Other Achievements······82
Chapter Eight The High and Late Middle Ages······85
  8.1 The High Middle Ages (1000–1300 AD)······85
    8.1.1 Pilgrimage (11th–12th Century)······86
    8.1.2 The Crusade······87
    8.1.3 Medieval Towns······88
    8.1.4 Fairs······89
  8.2 Gothic Architecture and Art······91
  8.3 Other Achievements······95
    8.3.1 Education and Learning······95
    8.3.2 Science and Technology······95
  8.4 Late Middle Ages······96
Chapter Nine Renaissance······99
  9.1 Socio-economic Background······100
    9.1.1 Italian Cities······100
    9.1.2 Patronage······103
  9.2 Humanism······104
  9.3 Development of the Renaissance······105
    9.3.1 Why Did Renaissance Start in Florence?······105
    9.3.2 The Renaissance in Rome······107
  9.4 Renaissance Architecture and Art······109
    9.4.1 The Early Renaissance Period in Florence······109
    9.4.2 The High Renaissance Period in Rome······113
    9.4.3 Cities and Dwellings······113
Chapter Ten The Seventeenth Century······120
  10.1 Socio-economic Background······120
    The Reformation······121
  10.2 Baroque Architecture and Art······122
  10.3 French Baroque······127
Chapter Eleven The Eighteenth Century······133
  11.1 Socio-economic Background······133
    The Enlightenment······134
  11.2 Rococo Art and Architecture······135
Chapter Twelve The Nineteenth Century······140
  12.1 Socio-economic Background······140
  12.2 Architecture and Arts······141
    12.2.1 Neoclassicism······142
    12.2.2 Utilitarian Structures of Iron and Glass······146
Chapter Thirteen The Twentieth Century······150
  13.1 Socio-economic Background······150
  13.2 Architecture and Art······151
    13.2.1 The Arts and Crafts Movement······152
    13.2.2 Art Nouveau······152
    13.2.3 Art Deco······156
    13.2.4 Difference and Similarity of the Art Movements······159
    13.2.5 Modernism······161
References······168

Chapter One   The Ancient Egyptian Culture

导读

　　金字塔为何诞生于古埃及？单纯而稳定恒久的自然环境与气候条件对古埃及文化与艺术的形成和发展有何影响？

　　古埃及的疆域主要局限于尼罗河谷，呈现一个纵向布局的生活空间，像是一条穿越沙漠南北的中轴线。这种空间形态对埃及神庙和法老陵墓的纵向布局形式有着重要影响。

　　茫茫沙漠中依水而居的古埃及人，在定期泛滥的尼罗河畔耕作，在相对封闭且永恒不变的地理环境中发现了"静穆的伟大"和"持久永恒的秩序"，形成了独特的"为来世而艺术"的埃及风格，他们创造了表现永恒与崇高的几何形体金字塔和巨柱顶立的神庙，对后来的西方建筑艺术产生了深远的影响。

　　恒久强盛的古埃及文明是地中海文明的摇篮，而地中海文明又是西方文明的源头。公元7世纪，埃及陷入阿拉伯帝国，从而成为伊斯兰文化的一部分。

　　We trace the origin of western civilization to ancient Egypt not only for its long recorded history, but also for its position as the cradle of the Mediterranean civilization, which in turn is the source of western civilization.

　　Egyptian civilization developed around 3150 BC with the political unification of Upper and Lower Egypt under the first pharaoh, establishing a capital at Memphis, from which the pharaohs could control the labor force and agriculture of the fertile delta region as well as the lucrative and critical trade routes to Western Asia. (Fig. 1.1)

　　In 332 BC, ancient Egypt was conquered by Alexander the Great, a Greek king of Macedonia. The city of Alexandria was established to showcase the power and prestige of Greek rule. It became a seat of learning and culture, centered at the famous Library of Alexandria, the largest and most significant library of the ancient world. The Lighthouse of Alexandria lit the way for the many ships which kept trade flowing through the city. (Fig. 1.2)

An Introduction to Western Culture and Art

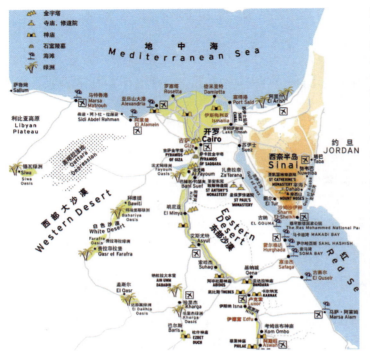

Fig. 1.1
On both sides of the long and narrow Nile valley are deserts which put clearly defined limits to man's space, making Egypt a longitudinal oasis. Egypt could be divided into Upper Egypt and Lower Egypt. In Upper Egypt, the valley is confined by ranges of mountains. In Lower Egypt the transition between oasis and desert is more gradual. Here great pyramids were placed to form a row of artificial mountains.

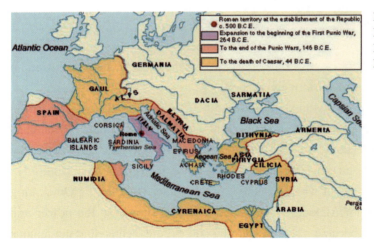

Fig. 1.2
Egypt fell to the Roman Empire and became a Roman province.

Fig. 1.3
Arab Empire in the 7th century permanently removed all of North Africa from the Western world.

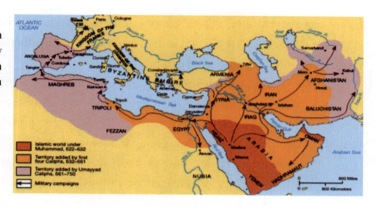

In 31 BC, Egypt fell to the Roman Empire and became a Roman province. The Romans relied heavily on grain shipments from Egypt. The obelisks and other relics were transported back to Rome. The Romans also imported building materials from Egypt to erect structures in Egyptian style. Alexandria became an increasingly important center on the trade route with the orient, as exotic luxuries were in high demand in Rome.

However, the Arab Empire in the 7th century permanently removed all of North Africa from the Western world and made it part of the Islamic Empire instead. (Fig. 1.3)

1.1 Geographical Environment

Egypt means "the gift of the Nile" in Latin. People in the expanse of desert had to have water and that's why the ancient Egyptians centered their lives along the Nile. On both sides of the long and narrow Nile valley are deserts which put clearly defined limits to man's space. The Egyptian landscape offers a first clue to a better understanding of the basic phenomena of Egyptian culture. Hardly any other country has a geographical structure of such simplicity and regularity. Every year, with the arrival of flood season (from July to November), the water would fill the man-made canals and water the crops for the coming year. The Egyptians were able to easily grow crops and vegetables in the fertile earth left after flooding and the fields on either side of Nile form a longitudinal oasis, with Nile flowing from south to north as the axis.

Egypt can therefore be described as a longitudinal oasis with a relatively uniform character throughout. Its climate is dry and stable, and together with regular flooding of the Nile, manifesting an eternal natural order.

In this setting, a sophisticated and creative society developed and endured for thousands of years. With deserts to the east and west, Mediterranean to the north and Nile's rapids to the south, natural barriers provided good protection against frequent hostile attacks for many centuries, giving it a sense of security and permanence.

Egypt could be divided into two sections: Upper Egypt and Lower Egypt. In Upper Egypt, the valley is confined by ranges of mountains. In Lower Egypt the transition between oasis and desert is more gradual, but clearly defined. Here great pyramids were placed to form a long row of artificial mountains parallel to the Nile. Therefore, the layout of Egyptian settlements and buildings were arranged in accordance with the great longitudinal space of the Nile valley.

1.2 Achievements in Art and Architecture

1.2.1 The Development of Pyramid

The regular floods and the relatively enclosed geographical environment accounted for the ancient Egyptian's belief of immortality and eternity. The arts of ancient Egypt were linked with this belief and maintained their unique character of "great calmness" "everlasting order" and "invariable ethics" that were observed in artistic creations and formed the Egyptian style that was characterized as "art for the next life". (Fig. 1.4)

The wish to present an eternal order in symbolic form implies a necessity to demonstrate the continuation of life after death. Tombs and mortuary temples, which are "houses of eternity", were therefore the primary building tasks of ancient Egypt. A pyramid is a tomb, a four-sided stone structure that symbolizes the sacred mountain, indicating man's universal striving to reach the heavens—the ancient belief in raising the human spirit towards the gods. Stone was selected for its hardness and resistance to decay, with its natural character enhanced through the contrasts of smooth surfaces and sharp edges, to achieve the effect of mass and weight. (Fig. 1.5) The pyramid, as a monumentalized version of the mastaba (bench) tomb and step pyramid, made the eternal presence of Pharaoh visible. The mastaba is a flat-roofed rectangular structure of mudbrick or stone built over an underground burial chamber. The step pyramid is a

Fig. 1.4
Art for the next life: Ramesses II (left), 1250BC, decoration of coffin(right)

Fig. 1.5
The contrasts of smooth surfaces and sharp edges are used to achieve the effect of mass and weight that symbolizes the sacred mountain.

Fig. 1.6
A pyramid is a series of stone mastabas stacked on top of each other over an underground burial chamber.

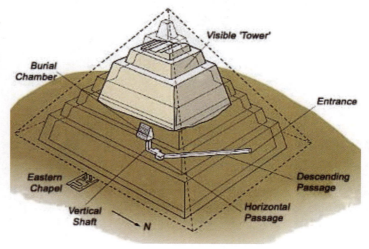

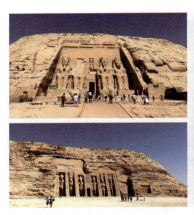
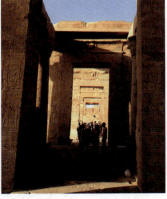

Fig. 1.7 (left)
The tombs were cut into the limestone rock.

Fig. 1.8 (right)
The rising sun, as the representative of Pharaoh was seen from the inside through its gateway, the "gate of heaven".

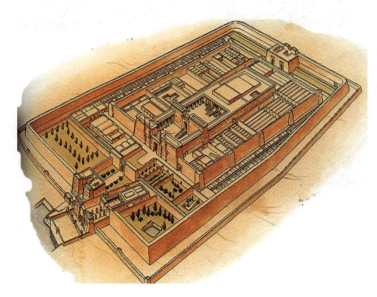

Fig. 1.9
Penetrating into the building, the spaces become gradually smaller. The floor rises and the ceiling drops down, creating a mystical atmosphere.

series of stone mastabas stacked on top of each other. (Fig. 1.6)

The spectacular pyramids, built in Old Kingdom (2755–2255 BC), that have made Egypt so famous are truly one of the world's greatest architectural wonders. The most famous pyramids are found at Giza, just west of Cairo. They are surrounded by smaller pyramids, mastabas (tombs of nobles), funerary temples, processional ramps and the Great Sphinx.

Pyramids were built during the Old and Middle Kingdoms, but later rulers abandoned them in favor of less conspicuous rock-cut tombs. As security against robbers, the pharaohs were now buried in rock-cut tombs hidden away in the river valley in the western desert behind the cliffs overlooking Thebes, sometimes tunneled as much as 150m into the hillside. The Valley of the King, famous for its beautifully painted royal tombs, is the world's most magnificent burial ground, built in New Kingdom (1570–1070 BC). The tombs were cut into the limestone rock in a remote dried-up river valley on the west side of the Nile, opposite the present day city of Karnak. Their walls were painted and sculpted with beautiful murals depicting scenes of daily life and the land of the gods. (Fig. 1.7)

1.2.2 Temple

The arrangement of the temple is symbolic. As the temples were generally oriented towards the east, the rising sun was seen from the inside through its monumental gateway, the "gate of heaven", through which emerged the shining sun-god and his representative, the Pharaoh. (Fig. 1.8) Basically the plan of the temple consists of three parts—a colonnaded courtyard, a hypostyle hall and a sanctuary—arranged along an axis, repeating the same structure of Egyptian nature and landscape on a small scale. (Fig. 1.9) In the larger temples there may be two courtyards and two or more halls, which are covered by ceilings decorated with painted stars, whereas the court is open to the sky and the sun. The main hall was usually lit from a central clerestory. Penetrating into the building, the spaces become gradually smaller. The floor rises and the ceiling drops down, with rows of columns acting as structural members, creating a mystical atmosphere. Finally, the sanctuary appears at the end of the axis, indicating the path of life.

1.2.3 Art

The ancient Egyptians produced art to serve its political and religious purposes with precision and clarity. For over 3500 years, artists adhered to artistic forms developed during the Old Kingdom, following a strict set of principles that resisted foreign influence and internal change. These artistic standards—simple lines, shapes, and flat areas of color (paints were obtained from minerals) —created a sense of order and balance within a composition. (Fig. 1.11)

Ancient Egyptian artisans used stone to carve statues and fine reliefs. Pharaohs

An Introduction to Western Culture and Art

Fig. 1.10 (left)
Model houses

Fig. 1.11 (right)
Simple lines, shapes, and flat areas of color

Fig. 1.12
Wooden, metal or clay models were made to depict scenes from everyday life and duplicate the activities of the living in the afterlife.

Fig. 1.13
Egyptian buildings were decorated with paintings, carved stone images and three-dimensional statues.

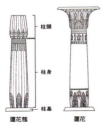   

Fig. 1.14
Plant motifs were used on the rich variety of columns which is derived from plant forms: the closed and open versions of papyrus, lotus and palm.

used reliefs to record victories in battle, religious scenes and etc. Wooden, metal or clay models were made to depict scenes from everyday life, and duplicate the activities of the living in the afterlife. These models show laborers, houses, boats, and even military formations that are scale representations of the ideal ancient Egyptian afterlife. (Fig. 1.10, Fig. 1.12)

Apart from the pyramids, Egyptian buildings were decorated with paintings, carved stone images and three-dimensional statues. (Fig. 1.13) Plant motifs were used on the rich variety of columns which is derived from plant forms: the closed and open versions of papyrus, lotus and palm, though they played a role as structural members. (Fig. 1.14)

Egyptian art tells the story of the pharaohs, the gods, the common people and the natural world of plants, birds and animals. Egyptians left thousands of illustrations depicting daily life in the Old Kingdom, but none of them show how pyramids were built. Therefore, how the ancient Egyptians were able to construct those massive structures using primitive tools is still a mystery.

New Words and Expressions

unification   *n.* 统一
pharaoh   *n.* 法老
fertile   *a.* 肥沃；富饶
delta   *n.* 三角洲
lucrative   *a.* 获利多的；赚钱的
Macedonia   *n.* 马其顿（希腊北部省份）
Alexandria   *n.* 亚历山大
showcase   *v.* 展示
prestige   *n.* 威望；声望
obelisk   *n.* 方尖碑
relic   *n.* 遗迹；废墟
exotic   *a.* 异国的；异国情调的
longitudinal   *a.* 纵向的；长度的
oasis   *n.* 绿洲
axis   *n.* 轴线

uniform *a.* 无变化的；统一的
manifest *v.* 清楚地表明；显示；证明
eternal *a.* 永远的；永恒的
sophisticated *a.* 复杂的；高级的
hostile *a.* 表现敌意的
permanence *n.* 永久性
confine *v.* 将某人/某物限制在一定范围以内
transition *n.* 过渡；转变
define *v.* 清楚地显示出（线条、形状、特征等）；画出……的轮廓
layout *n.* 安排；设计；布局
immortal *a.* 不朽的；永世的；流芳百世的
observe *v.* 遵守；奉行（法律、规则等）
mortuary *n.* 太平间
sacred *a.* 神圣的
monumentalize *v.* 使……伟大/宏伟；使……具有纪念意义
version *n.* 样式；种类；版本
stack *v.* 将某物堆起；垒起
spectacular *a.* 场面壮观的；引人入胜的
processional *a.* 宗教列队式的（used in a solemn religious procession）
ramp *n.* 人造斜坡；坡道
conspicuous *a.* 明显的；引人注目的
magnificent *a.* 宏伟的；壮观的
limestone *n.* 石灰石
mural *n.* 壁画
depict *v.* 描述；描绘；刻画
colonnade *n.* 列柱；柱廊（row of columns）
hypostyle *a.* 多柱式的（supported by columns）
         n. 多柱式建筑（a structure in which the ceiling is supported by columns）
sanctuary *n.* 圣所（holiest part of a temple or church）
clerestory *n.* 高窗
penetrate *v.* 进入或穿过某物
precision *n.* 明确性；精确性
adhere to 坚持/忠于某事物
composition *n.* （绘画、摄影）构图

artisan   *n.* 工匠 (craftsman)
statue   *n.* 雕像；塑像；铸像
relief   *n.* 深／浅浮雕
duplicate   *v.* 复制
three-dimensional   *a.* 三维的；立体的
motif   *n.* 主题；中心思想；基本图案；基调
papyrus   *n.* 纸莎草
lotus   *n.* 莲花
palm   *n.* 棕榈树
illustration   *n.* 插图；图表，图案；例证；实例

Chapter Two　Ancient Greek Culture

导读

　　从埃及北部越过地中海就到了希腊。然而，与统一专治的古埃及不同，古希腊不是一个统一的国家，而是散落在巴尔干半岛南部和爱琴海岛屿上的众多城邦，他们同属一个民族，享有同样的语言文化和宗教信仰。

　　对于古希腊人来说，一个理想的城邦包括位于城市制高点上与神庙相拥的卫城，供奉着他们的守护神，还有一个广场、一个剧场、一个运动场，以及数千名自由、勇敢和健美的市民。一个希腊城邦就是一个微型的国家。

　　走进希腊城邦，你才得以体验古希腊人的生活场景，赞叹古典柱式的完美比例与优美韵律、神庙的光影造型与雕塑感，见证古希腊如何开创了西方古典建筑艺术的时代。

　　希腊－罗马时代被后人称为古典时期，延续了大约一千年（5th BC-5th AD）。

2.1 Geographical Environment

　　To the north of Egypt, across the Mediterranean Sea, Greek landscape is characterized by a great variety of natural sites. The fertile valleys and plains are small, bounded by strong and barren mountains, which break up the country into many different states. The climate is dry. Intense sunlight and clear air give the forms an unusual presence.

　　Greece was not a unified country, but made up of hundreds of democratic city-states, scattered at the southern end of the Balkan Peninsula, on the islands in the Aegean Sea and along the western coastline of Asia Minor. (Fig. 2.1)

Fig. 2.1
Greece was not a unified country, but made up of democratic city-states.

2.2 Greek City-states

A typical city-state is in fact a city and the country around it, with an acropolis at the highest point of the town, having a population of no more than 50,000 people. Athens was the second largest city-state (Sparta was the largest) with more than 300,000 people at the height of power and splendor. Although these city-states were independent, they belonged to the same race and shared the same religion, tradition, language and epics. Contests of sports and poems as well as drama festivals were held regularly, which were enjoyed by people from all the city-states.

Unlike Sparta, the city-state of Athens became wealthy through trade with others, tributes from other dependent states, and a large slave-based economy. Athens was wealthy, many of its citizens had relatively large amount of leisure, and they enjoyed contact with the outside world. The city produced a remarkable series of writers,

14 An Introduction to Western Culture and Art

Fig. 2.2
An ideal city-state included an acropolis where they built their important temples and people could retreat to if under attack.

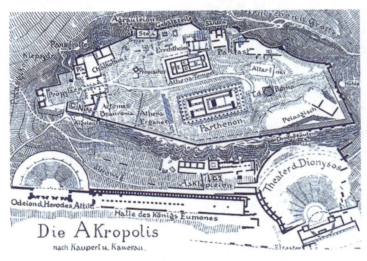

Fig. 2.3
Ground plan of Athenian Acropolis. The distribution of temples is irregular, and the arrangement of space outside the building is suitable for festivals and celebrations.

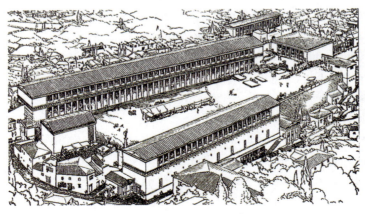

Fig. 2.4
The agora was the public place for social life, business and politics.

thinkers, philosophers, and politicians. They created democracy, invented theatre, and produced great art, architecture and literature. On the contrary, all Spartan citizens were full-time professional soldiers. As a result of lifetime training, the Spartans were famed for their military abilities.

2.3 The Achievements of Greek Culture

Greek culture reached a high point of development in the 5th century BC This was marked by the successful repulse of the Persian invasion early in the century, the establishment of democracy and the flourishing of science, philosophy, literature, architecture, and art in Athens. In 490 BC, when Persians launched an expedition against Greece, Athens took the lead in the allied forces of Greek city-states. The two armies met at Marathon in Attica and the Athenians defeated the invading army, which established the dominant position of Athens among the other city-states. For the Athenians, the battle at Marathon stood as their greatest military accomplishment. From then on, the Athenians began to think of themselves as the center of Greek culture and power. This pride was the foundation on which much of their cultural achievements were built. Therefore, the principle subject of their great dramas is the celebration of Athenian greatness. The great building projects were motivated by the need to display Athenian wealth, greatness and power.

After the war, taking advantage of the tributes from those city-states that looked to Athens' navy for protection, Athens was under a large-scale construction. These splendid building programs were directed by Perikles, the chief man in Athens then. The Classical Age of Greek culture began.

To ancient Greeks, an ideal city-state included an acropolis with temples and statues of the gods they worshiped, an agora, a theatre, a stadium and thousands of brave, strong and handsome citizens. Most city-states in ancient Greece had at their centre a rocky mound or hill where they built their important temples and where the people could retreat to if under attack. The Athenian Acropolis was adorned with world famous building, the Parthenon built for the goddess Athena. The bronze figure of Athena stood under the open sky, watching over Athens. The Acropolis was also the focus for the Athenian festival. (Fig. 2.2, Fig. 2.3)

The agora was the public place. Here men came together for social life, business and politics. (Fig. 2.4) It represented the new democratic way of life and the living

16 An Introduction to Western Culture and Art

Fig. 2.5
The Erechtheion
Greek architecture is represented only by ruins, and we can merely guess their original structure.

Fig. 2.6 (left)
Classical Orders
They furnish the proportion of human bodies, their strength and beauty.

Fig. 2.7 (right)
Athena

Fig. 2.8
Parthenon dominates the city of Athens. The temple resembles a sculpture in the round.

heart of the city. As Greek life was dominated by religion, it is not surprising that the temples of ancient Greece were the biggest and most beautiful. They also had a political purpose as they were often built to celebrate civic power and pride, or offer thanksgiving to the god or goddess of a city for success in war.

Ever since its great epoch during the fifth century BC, the name of Athens has been a token of the social and cultural achievement of Greek civilization. The Athenian citizens could spend their days worshiping the gods, participating in athletic exercises, sitting in the theater or discussing questions under the marble colonnades.

Sacred sites such as Delphi, Olympia and Corinth were built for religious festivals, which were usually athletic competitions. In fact, the first recorded athletic event in Greek history is that at the sacred site of Olympia in 776 BC. The tradition of the Olympic Games continued amazingly for over one thousand years, until banned by the Roman emperor in 393 AD.

2.4 The Achievements in Architecture and Art

Architecture developed intensively not only in Athens but in the whole Greek area. However, Greek architecture is represented only by ruins, some so complete that we can merely guess as to their original structure. (Fig. 2.5)

2.4.1 Classical Orders

To understand the beauty of Greek architecture, we should first learn something about its language—the so-called Classical Orders. In everything the Greeks loved beauty, and to them beauty meant order. Each man was well-trained to be beautiful both in body and mind. The Doric column furnishes the proportion of a man's body, its strength and beauty. The Ionic, on the other hand, is characterized by feminine slenderness, and its capital resembles graceful curling hair. The Corinthian, finally, imitates the slight figure of a girl with more graceful ornaments. (Fig. 2.6, Fig. 2.7)

2.4.2 Temple

The architecture of ancient Greece is generally associated with temples, which are often regarded as mere aesthetic objects and expressions of the wish for visual refinements. Common to all temples is their appearance as clearly defined, plastic bodies. They are not simple masses, but articulate structures where an external colonnade

18 An Introduction to Western Culture and Art

EARLY FORM OF HUT

LATER FORM OF HUT

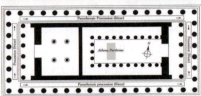

Fig. 2.9 (left)
Temples were developed from the mode of a house. Simple wooden pillars were developed into columns, made of marble or other stone.

Fig. 2.10 (right)
The interior space is rare.

Fig. 2.11
Sculpture on entablature on the Parthenon at display in the British Museum.

Fig. 2.12
Theatre was built on the slope of mountains in the form of a ring, with a platform in the bowl and the landscape behind serving as the background.

is of primary importance. The temple resembles a sculpture in the round—like a statue with its face on one side, so it is actively related to its site and to the purpose it has to serve—celebration and religious purpose. It was a static type of architecture: the visitor passed round a Greek temple, not through it. The emphasis was placed on its exterior rather than—as in Egypt—its interior. (Fig. 2.8)

Perhaps, the beauty of the temples has closed our eyes to other less conspicuous aspects of Greek architecture. However, temples were developed from the mode of a house. (Fig. 2.9) Simple wooden pillars were developed into columns, made of marble or other stone. The proportions were carefully worked out to achieve harmony. Its distribution seems irregular, and the interior space is rare, the arrangement of space outside the building is of special significance. The only feature common to all temples is a longitudinal cella which housed the statue of the god. (Fig. 2.10)

Of surviving monuments, none characterizes this Classical moment in Greek art better than the Parthenon, which still dominates the city of Athens and the surrounding country for many miles. Bold in outline, delicate in detail, majestically imposing, yet built to a scale of proportion so carefully regulated that it is not at all overpowering. Though sadly damaged (mainly in 1687) and robbed of most of its sculpture (now in the British Museum), it still retains the timeless quality of the building on the Acropolis over 2000 years after their erection. (Fig. 2.11)

2.4.3 Theatre

The theatre represents, next to the temple, the most important Greek contribution to the history of architecture. It was built on the slope of mountains in the form of a ring, with a platform embedded in the bowl and the landscape behind serving as the background. The spectators in their seats not only took part in the performance, but also experienced the surrounding landscape. (Fig. 2.12)

The Greek theatre history began with festivals honoring their gods. Men would go to the theatre for entertainment, to watch dramas that they could relate to, including tragedies and comedies, which often involved current politics and gods in some form. Greek dramas also told stories of the Greek heroes, so as to fill the people with noble thoughts. It is thought that women were not allowed to watch theatre or perform at the theatre, although male actors did play women roles.

Fig. 2.13
Greek Influence on 1893 Chicago World's Fair pavilions.

Fig. 2.14 (left)
Greek athlete, made around 50 AD. A copy of a bronze masterpiece around 320 BC.

Fig. 2.15 (middle)
Venus de Milo, 1st century BC.

Fig. 2.16 (right)
Apollo Belvedere, made around 2nd century AD. A copy of a masterpiece around 4th century BC.

Fig. 2.17
The original sculptures at the Erechtheion Temple.

Fig. 2.18
Many remaining sculptures are mutilated or exist only in fragments in the Britsh Museum.

Fig. 2.19
Greek Paintings

Fig. 2.20
Decorations on Greek pottery

2.5 Art and Sculpture

The art of ancient Greece has exercised an enormous influence on the culture of many countries from ancient times until the present, particularly in the areas of sculpture and architecture. In the West, the art of the Roman Empire was largely derived from Greek models. In the East, Alexander the Great's conquests initiated several centuries of exchange between Greek, Central Asian and Indian cultures. Following the Renaissance in Europe, the humanist aesthetic and the high technical standards of Greek art inspired generations of European artists. Well into the 19th century, the classical tradition derived from Greece dominated the art of the western world. (Fig. 2.13)

Greek art was almost entirely devoted to civic and religious purposes. In Greek art the gods took part in the human world, with the form, the dress and the behavior of men, so that the noble beauty of the human form became the most convincing image of the god. (Fig. 2.15, Fig. 2.16)

Greek Sculptures and carvings were made to represent each city state's heroes and past legends including animals and humans. Large temples were built in tribute to the Gods and were furnished with precious statues and art, as competition was fierce in the Greek world to surpass previous works of art. The growth of new trade routes and the opportunities for colonization permitted Greek art to flourish, and an amalgamation of Greek and oriental art.

Classical Art (480–323 BC) was created during a "golden age", from the time when Athens rose to prominence and Greek expansion. The Classical age could be seen as a turning point in art and produced some of the most exquisite sculptures known today. It was during this age that sculptors had mastered many different types of materials in their sculptures including stone, marble and limestone as these were abundant in Greece, and created statues that showed joyous freedom of movement and expression, and perfection in human form as well. (Fig. 2.14)

However, all the greatest works of sculpture admired by ancient Greek have vanished and many of those that remain are mutilated or exist only in fragments. (Fig. 2.17, Fig. 2.18) Buildings survive but in ruins and they have lost most, and sometimes all, of the decorations for which they were renowned. Of the vast number of bronze and marble statues described by ancient writers only a very few still exist, as bronzes were melted down, and marbles were converted into lime. Thus our knowledge of the most famous Greek works of art comes largely from written descriptions and Roman copies which are not always faithful to the original.

Like many people today, the Romans had a deep respect for Greek sculptures and many were copied. If the Romans had not made these copies, many of the Greek Legends and stories that we know today would have been lost to antiquity.

Paintings of the Classical period are known to have been copied in Italy and probably provide models for scenes depicted on the walls of houses at Pompeii. But there is no means of telling how faithful the copyists were. The only other visual

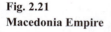
Fig. 2.21
Macedonia Empire

evidence we have is that provided by the decorations on Greek pottery, as unlike pottery, bronze and silver can be easily recycled. Yet great skill and artistry were lavished on them. Usually, the figures were shown in black on a light orange-red ground or vice versa. This was a Greek invention which called for great technical skill. (Fig. 2.19, Fig. 2.20)

2.6 The Fall of Greek Culture

Athens and Sparta were two rival city-states although at one time they had been united to protect the Greek states from a series of invasions by Persia. The victory over Persians left Athens with the most powerful fleet in the Aegean. Most of the Greek states looked upon Athens as the leading city and the cultural center of the Greek world, which spelled its downfall as the Spartans grew increasingly frightened of Athenian power and suspicious of Athenian intentions. Athens and Sparta came into conflict in 431 BC. The war ended in 404 BC with the defeat of Athens and its democracy.

Now Sparta became the greatest power in the Greek world, and further wars followed among the Greeks until they exhausted themselves. Meanwhile, the state of Macedonia to the north of Greece evolved as a great power and invaded Greece. In 338 BC, Greeks were defeated and came under the rule of Macedonia. The empire created by Alexander the Great spanned the entire coast of eastern Mediterranean and reached far into Asia, including Egypt, Asia Minor, the Middle East and India, spreading Greek language, art, architecture and literature throughout the Near East. (Fig. 2.21) This was the period of Hellenism, when the importance of Greek city-states within the Greek-speaking world declined sharply and Alexandria became the greatest city in the eastern Mediterranean. The Hellenistic Age ended in 30 BC when Egypt fell to Rome.

New Words and Expressions

bounded by　由……划界；限制
Balkan Peninsula　*n.* 巴尔干半岛
Aegean Sea　*n.* 爱琴海
Asia Minor　*n.* 小亚细亚
acropolis　*n.* 雅典卫城
splendor　*n.* 壮观；壮丽
epics　*n.* 史诗；叙事诗
tribute　*n.* 贡品；崇敬
repulse　*n.* 击退
expedition　*n.* 远征；探险（队）
accomplishment　*n.* 完成；成功；成就
agora　*n.* 古希腊城市广场和市场
mound　*n.* 小丘；小土冈
retreat　*v.* 撤退；退却
adorn　*v.* 装饰
Parthenon　*n.* 帕台农神庙
Goddess Athena　*n.* 雅典娜女神
watch over　*v.* 看护
civic　*a.* 城市的；公民的
epoch　*n.* 时代；纪元
token　*n.* 象征
marble colonnades　大理石柱廊
Classical Orders　古典柱式
furnish　*v.* 为房间配备家具或陈设；提供
Doric　多立克柱式
proportion　*n.* 比例
Ionic　爱奥尼克柱式
feminine　*a.* 女性气质的

slender   *a.* （人）瘦长的；苗条的
capital   *n.* （建筑）柱头
resemble   *v.* 相似；相像
Corinthian   科林斯柱式
slight   *a.* 纤细；纤弱
ornament   *n.* 装饰物
aesthetic   *a.* 美学的
refinement   *n.* 精炼；精制
plastic body   （雕）塑体
distribution   *n.* （人、物）分布；布局
cella   *a.* 内殿（a small room or inner part of an ancient Greek or Roman temple）
articulate   *a. & v.* 形成连接；连接完美
static   *a.* 静态的；不动的；不变化的
majestic   *a.* 雄伟；壮丽；崇高
imposing   *a.* 壮丽的；气势宏伟的
overpowering   *a.* 强烈的；不可抗拒的
embed   *v.* 嵌入；放入
amalgamation   *n.* 合并
erection   *n.* 建造；设立
exquisite   *a.* 精制的；精美的；优雅的；制作精良的
mutilate   *v.* （身体）伤残，断肢
fragment   *n.* 碎片；碎块
antiquity   *n.* 古代
artistry   *n.* 创作天资；艺术才华/技巧
lavish   *v.* 慷慨地给予
spell   *v.* 招致；带来（不愉快的结果）；意味
Macedonia   *n.* 马其顿
Hellenism   *n.* 古希腊及东地中海其他国家的历史、文化、艺术，古希腊文化、理想或精神

Chapter Three   Ancient Roman Culture

导读

　　与微型、完美和富有诗意的希腊城邦相比，罗马帝国追求雄伟宏大。罗马人具有强大的统治能力和建设能力。罗马人的组织能力和管理天才使其疆土跨越欧洲大部以及亚洲和非洲的部分地区，形成一个环绕地中海，囊括西方文明最发达地区的强大帝国。

　　罗马人最擅长的艺术是建筑，罗马艺术就体现在各种类型的大规模城市公共建筑群之中。罗马人不仅热爱希腊的雕塑与绘画，也迷恋希腊柱式。但是，两者的不同之处在于，希腊人运用单纯的梁柱结构表现了神庙的完美与崇高，罗马人则运用希腊柱式装饰其宏伟的构筑，创造空灵的空间感受；古希腊艺术重在表现建筑外部的雕塑感，古罗马艺术重在创造建筑宏大复杂的内部空间。

　　罗马人既不像埃及人那样以敬畏之心表现神的崇高，也不像希腊人那样用柱廊和山墙塑造神庙细腻优美的外部形象，罗马人运用水泥浇筑技术建造穹顶和拱券，创造出复杂的跨度和开敞的内部空间，从而创造了万神庙、斗兽场、大型浴场、城市广场、凯旋门、高架水渠等多种类型的城市公共建筑，因此，罗马人发展了建筑工程技术。

　　古希腊、古罗马建筑被誉为古典主义风格。

3.1 Geographical Environment

　　Ancient Rome was located exactly where modern Rome is today, along the western coast of central Italy. The city grew from settlements around a ford on the river Tiber, a crossroads of traffic and trade. Rome has its tremendous environmental advantages in that it is the natural location of the main north-south road in Italy, where it is easier to cross the Tiber, with an island in the river. Also riverboats going up and down the river, from east to west and back, could stop at Rome. (Fig. 3.1, Fig. 3.2)

Chapter Three Ancient Roman Culture   27

Fig. 3.1 (left)
The city grew from settlements, located on seven hills, around a ford on the river Tiber.

Fig. 3.2 (right)
Tiber Island (the ford) was connected to the two sides with small bridges.

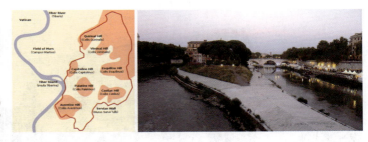

Fig. 3.3
A centralized network of roads. "All roads lead to Rome".

Whereas the Greek world consisted of a multitude of individual places, the Romans always centered on the capital, with its most conspicuous feature, a centralized network of roads. The capital city of Rome signified the idea of the Center, the nucleus of a well-ordered, disciplined and hierarchically organized authority. If the world could be conceived as a body, then Rome was its head.

The Romans mastered nature, technically and spatially, and their dominant system of roads manifested man's wish to conquer the world. The Romans were the greatest road builders who made roads from one colony to another. (Fig. 3.3) By these roads soldiers could march easily to any place where they were needed. In such a network, the nodes are particularly important, and the Romans gave them due attention by means of gateways and triumphal arches. (Fig. 3.4)

Fig. 3.4
Romans built gateways and triumphal arches at the important nodes of their road system.

Fig. 3.5
Rome was the greatest power on Earth, ruling Britain and the countries around the Mediterranean Sea.

Fig. 3.6 (left)
Plan of city Rome 31 BC–330 AD

Fig. 3.7 (right)
The Romans were mighty builders and Rome was adorned with beautiful buildings.

3.2 From Republic to Empire

According to the tradition, the Roman Republic was established around 509 BC. The small city-state was ruled by the Senate, an advisory council of the ranking nobility, which was presided over by two annually elected consuls. The two consuls together exercised executive authority.

From about the first to around the fifth century AD, Rome was the greatest power on Earth, ruling Britain and the countries around the Mediterranean Sea, through conquest and assimilation. (Fig. 3.5) The conquests of the Romans had made them rich, and care more about wealth and luxury. The Romans were mighty builders and Rome was adorned with beautiful buildings. The citizens were amused by games and sports.

The imperial city of Rome was the largest urban center of its time, with a population of about one million people (about the size of London in the early 19th century, when London was the largest city in the world). Life in ancient Rome revolved around the city of Rome, located on seven hills. The city had a vast number of monumental structures like the Forum, the Pantheon, the Colosseum, theaters, gymnasiums, and bath complexes complete with libraries and shops. It also had fountains with fresh drinking-water supplied by hundreds of miles of aqueducts, functional sewers, and marketplaces. (Fig. 3.6, Fig. 3.7)

Different types of outdoor and indoor activities and entertainment were available. The Forum was the central business district, where most of the Romans would go for marketing, shopping, trading, and for participating in festivities and ceremonies. The Forum was also a place where orators would express themselves to mould public opinion, and elicit support. (Fig. 3.8, Fig. 3.9, Fig. 3.10)

Huge crowds would gather at the Colosseum to watch events like combats between men, or fights between men and the wild animals. (Fig. 3.11)

Romans were particularly famous for their public baths, which were used for both hygienic and social purposes. Every Roman city had its bath buildings. As most of the houses did not have running water, baths were extremely important, both in terms of social and practical needs, and they served as a place for social interaction. Romans made major advancements in sanitation.

In the provinces of the Roman Empire, forums, temples, bath buildings, amphitheaters and apartment blocks were built, though generally on a smaller scale

Fig. 3.8
The city had a vast number of monumental structures like the Forum(front), Triumphal Arches(right), Colosseum(right), Basilica(left), etc.

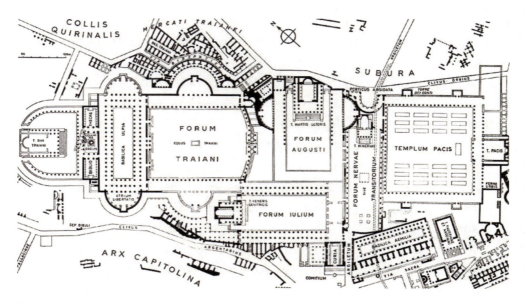

Fig. 3.9
The Forum was the central business district, for marketing, trading, festivities and ceremonies.

Chapter Three Ancient Roman Culture 31

**Fig. 3.10
The market at Forum of Trajan**

**Fig. 3.11
Inside Colosseum**

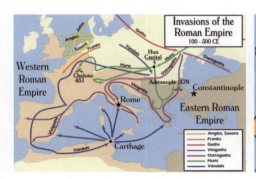

Fig. 3.12
There were now two great centers in Roman Empire, the new capital Constantinople in the east and the old capital Rome in the west.

Fig. 3.13
The Empire was permanently divided into the Eastern Roman Empire (later known as the Byzantine Empire) and the Western Roman Empire in 395.

than those in Rome. The provinces too were well governed. There are many well-preserved Roman cities around the Roman Empire.

Governing a vast territory, the Romans developed the science of public administration to an extent never before conceived or necessary, creating an extensive civil service. The Roman contribution to the form of government has influenced various constitutions including those of most European countries and many former European colonies.

From the third century AD the empire began to suffer a number of great crises, civil wars, attacks on the frontiers, invasions by fierce tribes and other problems. In order to better administer and defend the vast territory, in the late third century AD, Emperor Diocletian appointed separate rulers for the eastern and western parts of the empire. In 330, Emperor Constantine I moved the capital to the Greek city of Byzantium in the east, renaming it Constantinople, which was easier to defend than Rome. There were now two great centers in the empire, with very different backgrounds and cultures—the new capital, Constantinople, in the east and the old capital, Rome, in the west. The Empire was permanently divided into the Eastern Roman Empire (later known as the Byzantine Empire) and the Western Roman Empire in 395. (Fig. 3.12, Fig. 3.13)

The Western Roman Empire went into decline and disappeared in the 5th century AD. Plagued by internal instability and attacked by various barbarians, the western part of the empire, broke up into independent kingdoms in the 5th century, and the rule of Rome in the West came to an end. However, in the west, Latin continued to be used by scholars and the church right through the Middle Ages and well into the seventeenth century.

The eastern part of the empire, with Greek as its language, became what modern historians now call the Byzantine Empire. However, the Empire was never called thus by its inhabitants, who still saw themselves as Romans, and their state as the rightful successor to the ancient empire of Rome. Byzantine Empire survived and continued until 1453, when its last remains were finally annexed by the emerging Turkish Ottoman Empire.

3.3 Roman Technological Achievements

Ancient Rome commanded a vast area of land, with tremendous natural and human resources. The invasion of Greece and North Africa had a major cultural impact

Fig. 3.14
A row of purely decorative columns in front of a load-bearing wall, tile-covered concrete supplanted marble as the primary building material.

Fig. 3.15
Concrete's strength freed the floor plan from rectangular cells to a more free-flowing environment.

Fig. 3.16
A church converted from a Roman bath

on Rome. Treasures poured in, together with large numbers of Greek scholars, teachers, artists and slaves. Ancient Rome boasted impressive technological feats, using many advancements that would be lost in the Middle Ages, not be rivaled again until the 19th and 20th centuries.

Roman engineering as well as Roman military engineering constituted a large portion of Rome's technological superiority and legacy, and contributed to the construction of hundreds of roads, bridges, aqueducts, baths, theaters and arenas.

Roman engineers developed methods for city building on a grand scale. In the first century BC, Romans started to use concrete widely, a strong and readily available substitute for stone. Though concrete had been invented much earlier in the Near East, the Romans extended its use to their most impressive buildings and monuments, capitalizing on the material's strength and low cost. Massive buildings like the Pantheon, "Temple of all the gods", and the Colosseum could never have been constructed with previous materials and methods.

The freedom of concrete also inspired the colonnade screen, a row of purely decorative columns in front of a load-bearing wall. Concrete's strength freed the floor plan from rectangular cells to a more free-flowing environment. Tile-covered concrete quickly supplanted marble as the primary building material and more daring buildings soon followed, with great pillars supporting broad arches and domes. (Fig. 3.14, Fig. 3.15)

Because of these methods, Roman architecture is particularly renowned for the durability of its construction, with many buildings still standing, and some still in use, mostly buildings converted to churches during the Christian era. (Fig. 3.16) Their survival is testimony to the durability of their materials and design. Many ruins, however, have been stripped of their marble veneer and are left with their concrete core exposed, thus appearing somewhat reduced in size and grandeur from their original appearance.

Concrete made possible the paved, durable Roman roads many of which were still in use a thousand years after the fall of Rome. The construction of a vast and efficient travel network throughout the Empire dramatically increased Rome's power and influence. It was originally constructed to allow Roman armies to be rapidly deployed, however the road system had enormous economic significance, solidifying Rome's role as a trading crossroads—the origin of the saying "All roads lead to Rome". There was a very large amount of commerce between the provinces of the Roman Empire since its transportation technology was very efficient.

Chapter Three　Ancient Roman Culture　35

Fig. 3.17
The Pantheon

Fig. 3.18
Large dome

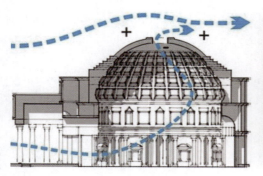

Fig. 3.19
Structure of the Pantheon

Fig. 3.20
In the Pantheon Roman architects for the first time created space by grand interior means of vaults and domes.

Fig. 3.21
The arch set before the altar in a church

The Romans constructed numerous aqueducts to supply water to cities and to assist their agriculture. Most aqueducts were constructed below the surface, with small portions above ground supported by arches.

3.4 Art and Architecture

Roman civilization is often grouped into "classical antiquity" with ancient Greece, a civilization that inspired much of the culture of ancient Rome. Many practical Roman innovations were adopted from earlier Greek designs, and many Roman homes were decorated with landscapes by Greek artists.

While the architecture of ancient Greece is generally associated with temples, the architecture of ancient Rome involves a multitude of building types, such as the grandiose structures of basilicas, amphitheatres, circuses and triumphal arches which in part were unknown prior to Roman times.

Greek building concentrated on the external appearance, and is generally perceived as "large sculpture" like the Parthenon. In contrast, Roman architecture for the first time created grand interior spaces and complex groups of spaces covered by vaults and domes such as the imposing public structures of the Pantheon, the Baths of Diocletian and the Baths of Caracalla. Therefore, the chief Roman contributions to architecture were the arch and dome. The Roman use of arch together with their construction of vaulted ceilings enabled huge public spaces such as basilicas. The Pantheon (built in 2nd century AD) is practically the only edifice of Roman age preserved intact throughout the centuries. The real wonder is the gigantic dome-shaped covering over a circular hall, with a central opening (of a diameter of about 9m), allowing for natural lighting and airflow. (Fig. 3.17, Fig. 3.18, Fig. 3.19, Fig. 3.20) It is referable for its typology to the structure of the calidarium of Roman bath complex. It served as a prototype of several other great buildings of Western architecture. This symbol of power was transformed and utilized within the Christian basilicas, with the arch set before the altar to symbolize the triumph of Christ and the after life. (Fig. 3.21)

Romans adopted the external language of classical Greek architecture, but used them in a fundamentally new way. What had been structural elements in Greek architecture became surface decoration in Roman architecture, where Doric, Ionic, and Corinthian columns are placed above each other. These Classical orders were combined with rustication to make walls. (Fig. 3.22) Therefore, instead of the trabeated systems of the Egyptian and Greek architecture, Roman concrete buildings consist of

Chapter Three   Ancient Roman Culture   37

Fig. 3.22
Doric, Ionic, and Corinthian columns are placed above each other to make colonnade screen as surface decoration in Roman Architecture.

Fig. 3.23
Roman basilica. Roman concrete buildings consist of a continuous system of vaults, arches, walls and pillars.

Fig. 3.24 (left)
Romans could build theaters anywhere, as they used concrete to build a hill, upon which they could support the seats.

Fig. 3.25 (right)
Rows of arches and vaults supporting seats at different levels.

Fig. 3.26 (left)
The arrangement of the seats.

Fig. 3.27 (right)
Greeks built their theaters on hillsides, as they used the natural hill to support the seats.

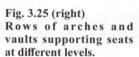
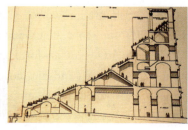 

a continuous system of vaults, arches, walls and pillars. That is the third distinguishing property of Roman architecture. (Fig. 3.23)

The Greeks always built their theaters on hillsides, as they used the natural hill to support the seats. The Romans wanted to build their theaters wherever they wanted to, and what they did was to use concrete to build a hill, upon which they could support those seats. And that's again a Roman innovation. (Fig. 3.24, Fig. 3.25, Fig. 3.26, Fig. 3.27)

With regard to city planning, the Greek grid pattern for cities was adopted by the Romans. Roman cities were well planned, efficiently managed and neatly maintained. In the Roman world, streets intersect at right angles, and the main streets lead to four gates in the city wall. From the very beginning, Rome was organized for war and the layout of the city resembled a Roman military camp.

At the heart of a city, large public squares, or forums were created. Here there would be a temple or temples, and a basilica, the place where public or administrative business was conducted. The forum would be surrounded by colonnades to keep off the sun. Nearby there would be other public buildings for entertainment and relaxation, such as baths surrounded by gardens with statues, shops and the like, even a library. City planning was comprehensive with provisions for different activities by the urban resident population. (Fig. 3.28)

Possibly, the most impressive, from an urban planning point of view, were the multi-story apartment blocks built to cater for a wide range of situations. The accumulation of wealth and high population densities in cities forced the ancient Romans to develop new architectural solutions of their own. Residential architecture ranged from very modest houses to country villas. In the capital city of Rome, there were private dwellings, villas, and elaborately designed imperial residence called palace. The vast majority of the population lived in the city center, packed into apartment blocks. These buildings solely intended as large scale accommodation could reach several floors in height. (Fig. 3.30)

While traditional view suggests that the ancient Roman art is often borrowed from Greek precedents (much of the Greek sculpture known today is in the form of Roman marble copies), as trade in art was brisk throughout the empire, and much of the Greek artistic heritage found its way into Roman art. Many art forms and methods used by the Romans—such as high and low relief, sculpture, mosaic, portrait painting, landscape painting, architectural sculpture, and etc.—all were developed or refined by Ancient Greek artists. But more recent analysis has indicated that Roman art is a highly creative

Chapter Three　Ancient Roman Culture　　39

Fig. 3.28
Remains of the city center

Fig. 3.29
Wall paintings

Fig. 3.30
Colonnade screen as a decoration for a multi-story apartment block

Fig. 3.31
Roman sculpture and relief

Fig. 3.32
Roman mosaics. National Museum of Roman Art, Merida Spain

pastiche relying heavily on Greek models but also encompassing native Italic, and even Egyptian visual culture.

Roman art was commissioned, displayed, and owned in far greater quantities, and adapted to more uses than in Greek times. Wealthy Romans were more materialistic; they decorated their walls with art, their homes with decorative objects, and themselves with fine jewelry. Sculpture was perhaps considered as the highest form of art by Romans, but portrait painting and mosaics were also very highly regarded. (Fig. 3.29, Fig. 3.31, Fig. 3.32)

The main innovation of Roman painting compared to Greek art was the development of landscapes, in particular incorporating techniques of perspective, though true mathematical perspective developed 1,515 years later. Some landscapes were pure scenes of nature, particularly gardens with flowers and trees, while others were architectural vistas depicting urban buildings. Of the vast body of Roman painting we now have only a few survivals. The best known and most important painting is the wall paintings from Pompeii, and other sites nearby, which show how residents of a wealthy seaside resort decorated their walls.

When Constantine moved the capital of the empire to Byzantium (renamed Constantinople), Roman art incorporated Eastern influences to produce the Byzantine style of the late empire. When Rome was sacked in the 5th century, artisans moved to and found work in the Eastern capital. The Church of Hagia Sophia in Constantinople employed nearly 10,000 workmen and artisans.

Because of the Empire's vast extent and long endurance, Roman influence upon the language, religion, philosophy, art and architecture, law and government of nations around the world lasts to this day, and its history continues to have a major influence on the modern world.

New Words and Expressions

ford　　*n.* 浅滩
a multitude of　　众多；大量
hierarchy　　*n.* 等级制度
node　　*n.* 节点；结点
triumphal arches　　*n.* 凯旋门
ranking　　*a.* 地位高的；高级的
preside　　*v.* 主持；负责
consul　　*n.* （古罗马共和国）二执政官之一
assimilation　　*n.* 同化
mighty　　*a.* 强有力的
be adorned with　　装饰
revolve　　*vi.* 旋转；环绕；围绕
monumental structures　　纪念性建筑
forum　　*n.* （古罗马的）广场／市场
Pantheon　　*n.* 万神殿
Colosseum　　*n.* 斗兽场
aqueduct　　*n.* 高架水渠
sewer　　*n.* 污水管；下水道
festivity　　*n.* 欢庆；庆典
orator　　*n.* 演说者；演讲人
mould　　*v.* 造型；影响……发展
elicit　　*vt.* 引出；诱出；探出
hygienic　　*a.* 卫生的；保健的
sanitation　　*n.* 公共卫生（设施）
amphitheater　　*n.* 露天圆形剧场／竞技场
Byzantium　　*n.* 拜占庭
plague　　*vt.* 折磨；不断困扰
annex　　*vt.* 吞并；霸占
Turkish Ottoman Empire　　土耳其奥斯曼帝国
feat　　*n.* 功绩

arena　*n.* （供运动、娱乐等的）活动场所；竞技场
concrete　*n.* 混凝土
capitalize on　利用
load-bearing wall　承重墙
rectangular　*n.* 矩形的
tile-covered　铺（贴）瓦或瓷砖的
supplant　*vt.* 取代
testimony　*n.* 证据；证明
be stripped of　剥去；除去
veneer　*n.* 饰面薄板；镶板
grandeur　*n.* 壮丽；壮观
deploy　*vt.* 部署；调动
classical antiquity　古代经典
grandiose　*a.* 浮夸的；华而不实的
basilica　*n.* 巴西利卡；长方形柱廊大厅／教堂（a church or hall with a curved end and with two rows of columns inside）
vault　*n.* 拱顶（a roof or ceiling made out of a number of arches, as in many churches）
referable to　*a.* 可参考的
typology　*n.* 类型学
calidarium　*n.* （罗马浴场）热水室
prototype　*n.* 原型；雏形
altar　*n.* 祭坛（a table or raised level surface used in a religious ceremony）
rustication　*n.* 粗面石工
trabeated　横梁式
grid　*n.* 方格
precedent　*n.* 先例
brisk　*a.* 轻快的；活泼的
mosaic　*n.* 马赛克；镶嵌工艺／画
portrait painting　*n.* 肖像画
pastiche　*n.* 拼凑的艺术品；混合而成的作品
encompass　*vt.* 包含；包括；涉及
commission　*vt.* 委托；委约
perspective　*n.* 透视（图）
vistas　*n.* 长条形景色；远景
sack　*vt.* 劫掠；毁坏
Hagia Sophia　*n.* 圣索菲亚大教堂

Chapter Four Early Christianity

导读

　　基督教诞生于巴勒斯坦地区，并于公元一二世纪在罗马帝国各地传播。基督教虽然屡遭残酷迫害，却具有顽强的生命力，苦难深重的基督徒只能聚集于陋室或地下举行礼拜仪式。公元4世纪，基督教成为罗马帝国的国教。当基督教堂得以大规模修建时，却找不到可以仿效的范例，只有在希腊罗马的古典柱式中寻找灵感。从此，西方建筑与艺术开始与教堂融为一体。

　　一种流行于希腊罗马时期、位于城市广场上的长方形大厅（原本用作市场和法庭），"巴西利卡"，正好适应了基督徒做礼拜的需要，成为早期基督教堂的原型。这种巴西利卡结构简单，中间是长方形中庭，两侧各有一低矮狭窄的侧廊，中庭与侧廊之间有一排古典列柱分隔，列柱通向中庭尽头有一个半圆形高台，顶部用半穹顶覆盖，那里曾经是会议主持人或法官的席位，现已成为基督教堂的圣坛，用马赛克壁画和彩色玻璃装饰，那是基督徒的精神归依之处。中庭两侧的古典柱式排列突出与强化了这条精神通道慢慢延伸，通向天国，两侧柱廊上方排列的高窗投进天光，照亮中庭，教堂简朴的外表与丰富的内心世界得以诠释，这正是早期基督教艺术的精髓所在。从此，巴西利卡成为基督教堂的代名词。

　　随着罗马帝国的灭亡，城市文明也随之消亡，城市的基础设施、贸易往来和文化传统遭到破坏。有些地方的城市文明依然得以延续，那是因为当地教堂已经成为地方实际的管理者，教会掌控着社会生活的方方面面。基督教在吸收罗马传统与文化的同时，不断发展演变，成为罗马帝国灭亡后西方文明发展的基石。

　　With the expansion of Roman territory, some mysterious religions flooded into the Empire. Christianity was a religion that originated in the first century in the Levant (now Palestine and Israel, then a part of the Roman Empire), and spread initially from Jerusalem throughout the Near East, then widely in the Roman world. The number of Christians had been steadily growing among all classes of people. Humble churches

Fig. 4.1
Christianity originated in the first entury in the Levant (now Palestine and Israel, then a part of the Roman Empire)

Fig. 4.2
Humble church underground. To escape from persecution early Christians lived in underground caves.

were built everywhere. Some collective worship even took place in private houses of some Christian families who were better off and whose houses were therefore larger. House churches of this kind ended up being donated to the Church. (Fig. 4.1, Fig. 4.2)

The Romans were tolerant of other religions, and paid little attention to the Christians at first. However, as it became evident that Christians cared more to obey God and defied emperor worship, the Roman authorities began to change their attitude toward them, considering Christianity illegal organization. The third century witnessed systematic persecution of Christians, which was most severe in the fourth century.

However, when the emperor Constantine (306–337 AD) recognized the power of Christianity he adopted it as a unifying force. He financed or built churches, converted temples to Christian use. He considered himself the head of the church. From then on, the church became associated with power. Bishops were given wealth and power as magistrates and linked to the court. In 392 AD, Christianity became the state religion of the Empire and it triumphed at last over all its rival faiths.

In 395 AD, the Empire was permanently divided into the Eastern Empire and the Western Empire, the latter broke up into independent kingdoms in 476 AD. Gradually, the Christian world was split, in 11th century, between the Catholic Church, centered in Rome and dominant in the West, and the Orthodox Church, centered in Constantinople, capital of the Byzantine Empire.

With the rise of Christianity in the midst of the Roman world, much of Rome's tradition and culture were absorbed by the new religion, and transformed into

Chapter Four　Early Christianity　45

Fig. 4.3
A Christian town was characterized by its churches and monastic buildings.

Fig. 4.4
Painting

Fig. 4.5
Mosaic

something new, which would serve as the basis for the development of Western civilization after the fall of Rome. The Roman Catholic Church, the only centralized institution to survive the fall of the Western Roman Empire, was the sole unifying cultural influence in the West.

4.1 Church and Monasticism

Jerusalem was the first center of the Christian church. In 66, the Jews revolted against Rome. The Roman army besieged Jerusalem for four years, and the city fell in 70. The city was destroyed, including the Temple, and the population was mostly killed or removed. With churches in other cities gradually assuming their independence, and more Latin-speaking people converted to Christianity, the center of Christian world shifted gradually to Rome. In Rome, in the 5th century AD, the construction of churches had an intensity that would be repeated until the seventeenth century. The city soon became the center of Christianity, especially when the Pope resided there.

The church has been the leading building task of European architects for centuries. Whereas Greek and Roman towns had a more complex appearance, the Christian town was characterized by its churches and monastic buildings, and castles sometimes formed another focus. Even today most European towns are dominated by a centrally located church which gives visible structure and meaning to the townscape. (Fig. 4.3)

4.1.1 Early Christian Architecture and Art (100–500 AD)

Early Christian art and architecture is the art produced by Christians or under Christian patronage from about the year 100 to about the year 500. It is hard to know when distinctly Christian art began. Prior to 100, Christians may have been constrained by their position as a persecuted group from producing durable works of art. The lack of surviving art may reflect a lack of funds for patronage, and small numbers of followers. After about 500 Christian art shows the beginning of Byzantine artistic style.

The artistic media of Early Christian art included paintings, fresco, mosaics, sculpture, manuscript illumination and etc. Images of Jesus and narrative scenes from the Life of Christ are the most common themes. (Fig. 4.4, Fig. 4.5) The largest groups of Early Christian paintings come from the tombs in the Catacombs of Rome, and show the evolution of the depiction of Jesus, since the conventional appearance of Jesus in

Chapter Four　Early Christianity　　47

Fig. 4.6
A typical Christian church has a center nave with one aisle at each side and an apse at one end, and the central nave is taller than the aisles.

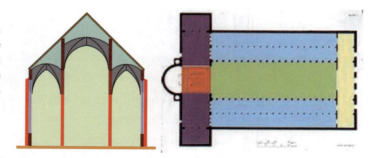

Fig. 4.7
The summary treatment of church exterior: Church of Santa Maria Rome.

Fig. 4.8
The continuous colonnades accompanying the nave emphasized the longitudinal movement, achieving the rich "heavenly" interior.

Fig. 4.9
Early Christians got inspiration and materials for their church from ancient Greek and Roman buildings. As indicated, this church reuses ancient Roman columns, with columns and capitals coming from different classical buildings.

art has remained remarkably consistent. Mosaics in churches in Rome are the most prominent surviving examples.

In the 4th century, once Christianity had been legalized, Christians were prepared to build larger and more handsome edifices for worship than the furtive meeting places they had been using. The architectural formulas for temples were unsuitable. The usable model at hand was the familiar conventional basilicas, which had a center nave with one aisle at each side and an apse at one end: on the raised platform sat the bishop and priests. (Fig. 4.6) In most basilicas the central nave is taller than the aisles, forming a row of windows called a clerestory. Therefore, from the very beginning, Christian churches consisted of two major parts: the congregational nave and the chancel placed at the east end.

The early Christian churches were conceived as interior worlds, and a pronounced interiority is common to all early churches. The summary treatment of church exterior was interpreted as a shell around a richly articulate interior. The concepts of "center" and "path" are symbolic meanings taken by the Early Christian architecture, indicating the directed human action. The continuous colonnades accompanying the nave emphasized the longitudinal movement, achieving the rich "heavenly" interior. By building the centre and the path as a church, the meaning of Christian space was made visible. (Fig. 4.7, Fig. 4.8)

Central and longitudinal spaces have already been found among the most significant Roman architecture, the centralized space of the Pantheon and the longitudinal spaces of Roman basilicas. Both forms were taken over by Early Christian architecture, and the plan of most early churches tended toward a combination of long rectangular space and centralized space; the former being dominant in the West Empire and the latter in the East Empire. (Fig. 4.10, Fig. 4.11) The Hagia Sophia presents a good combination of central and longitudinal structures.

The basic intention of Early Christian architecture is the creation of spiritualized space, which is achieved by means of a particular treatment of the surface of walls and a particular illumination. The nave is divided into two distinct zones: a tall upper wall resting on a row of columns. The upper zones are well lit, whereas the lower remain dim. The use of arcade makes the wall appear as one continuous surface. Arched clerestory windows light the nave and the transept, and the aisles remain dark. With the introduction of glass mosaic the walls were transformed into a shimmering skin. The directed basilica is of primary importance, as it combines spiritualized space with the

Chapter Four Early Christianity 49

Fig. 4.10
Long rectangular space

Fig. 4.11
Centralized space
The first house churches and the Baptistery of St. John Lateran in Rome

An Introduction to Western Culture and Art

Fig. 4.12
A combination of long rectangular space and centralized space San Andrea Della Valle Church, Rome (1590–1650).

Fig. 4.13
A monastery is an enclosure.

great theme of the path of life as a road to salvation. In the decorative arts, mosaics of Christian theme replace paintings as main part of early Christian art. (Fig. 4.12)

4.1.2 Introduction of Monasticism

The Early Middle Ages witnessed the rise of monasticism in the west. The traditions and ideas of monasticism originated in the deserts of Egypt and Syria, where those who rejected a painful or sinful world would seek community experience of the spiritual life. After Christianity was legalized in the Roman Empire, members of the church greatly increased, but religious moralities deteriorated. To withdraw from the real world and its temptations, some people abandoned their wealth and worldly pleasure, and moved into the desert. They chose to live a life isolated from human society in order to dedicate themselves wholeheartedly to the service of God. Some other Christians followed. Then in Egypt emerged the first monastic communities, characterized by routines of private prayer, group worship and physical work. Monastic ideals spread from Egypt to Western Europe in the 5th and 6th centuries and influenced European monasticism.

A monastery is an enclosure around a centrally placed church, consisting of cells, refectory, kitchen and guest house. As an "orderly and peaceful island within a society", silence, humility and asceticism reigned within the enclosure. The monks there lived a stable and peaceful life. They provided shelter for pilgrims and other travelers, copied manuscripts, taught others to read and write, prepared medicine, and helped the poor and the sick. Monasticism made a vital contribution to the economic and cultural development of medieval civilization. (Fig. 4.13)

New Words and Expressions

defy *vt.* 公然反抗；拒绝服从
Bishop *n.* 主教
magistrate *n.* 地方行政官
triumph *vt.* 战胜
the Orthodox Church *n.* 东正教
besiege *vt.* 包围；围攻
assume *vt.* 承担；采用

convert   *vt.* 转化；改变信仰
monastic   *a.* 修道院的；寺院的
mosaic   *n.* 镶嵌图案；马赛克
manuscript illumination   *n.* 金银粉饰面的手稿 / 花饰
narrative   *a. & n.* 叙述的；叙述
catacomb   *n.* 地下墓穴
edifice   *n.* 宏伟建筑；大厦
furtive   *a.* 偷偷摸摸的；鬼鬼祟祟的；遮遮掩掩的
nave   *n.* 教堂正厅（the long central part of a church）
aisle   *n.* 侧廊（a passage leading through the length of a church and divided from the nave）
apse   *n.* 教堂东端的半圆形小室（a small area, often in the shape of a semicircle, at the east end of the church）
clerestory   *n.* 天窗；高侧窗
congregation   *n.* 人群；会众（people gathered together in a church for religious worship）
chancel   *n.* （唱诗班牧师就座的）高坛（the eastern part of a church near the altar, where the priests sit during services）
pronounced   *a.* 明显的；显著的
articulate   *a.* 连接清晰的（having apparent joints）
Hagia Sophia   圣索菲亚大教堂
arcade   *n.* 拱廊（a covered passage with a roof supported by arches）
transept   *n.* 十字形教堂的耳堂（the part of a cross-shaped church that crosses the main body of a church at right angles）
shimmer   *vt.* 闪烁；闪光
salvation   *n.* 拯救
monasticism   *n.* 禁欲主义；修道院生活
deteriorate   *vt.* 使恶化；变坏
enclosure   *n.* 圈占地；圈用地；围场（a piece of land that is surrounded by a fence or wall and is used for a particular purpose）
refectory   *n.* 犹指英国教会团体和学校的食堂；餐厅（a large room in which meals are served, especially in a religious institution and in some schools and colleges in Britain）
humility   *n.* 谦逊
ascetic   *a.* 禁欲主义的；苦行生活的
pilgrim   *n.* 朝圣者

Chapter Five   The Early Middle Ages

导读

　　欧洲中世纪通常指从西罗马帝国灭亡（公元476年）至奥斯曼人征服君士坦丁堡、东罗马帝国灭亡（公元1453年），这段千年历史长河将罗马帝国的辉煌与意大利文艺复兴的璀璨分隔开来。这一时期又可细分为三个历史阶段：中世纪早期、中期和晚期。

　　中世纪早期（公元5世纪—10世纪）是一个蛮族侵略、战争频发、经济崩溃、社会破败的时代，与古希腊、古罗马文明形成天壤之别，因而被称为"黑暗的中世纪"。正是在这一时期形成了以天主教为核心的西欧文化，以东正教为标志的拜占庭文化和以穆罕穆德为先知的盛行于中东、北非、西班牙的伊斯兰文化。这三种文明在不同程度和不同领域吸收和传承了古典文明。中世纪开启了欧洲历史的新篇章。

　　在西欧，天主教会已经成为处理地方事务的管理机构，主教成为教皇，是实际的统治者。教堂和修道院成为学习与研究的中心，教士或牧师是当时的知识分子，他们的学习研究主要出于实际生活的需要：研究医药是为了照顾体弱多病者；研究数学和星球运动是为了计算复活节等宗教活动的时间。因此，从某种意义上说，教堂在保持和传承古典文化与艺术方面发挥了重要作用。

　　随着朝圣在欧洲的兴起，在朝圣的主要道路上巍然屹立的教堂和修道院拔地而起，为来往的朝圣者提供食宿和祈祷场所。此时，罗马的工程技术早已失传，只有少数残留的建筑可作参考。为了建造规模宏大的教堂，古罗马的拱顶技术被重新挖掘利用，以半圆形拱券结构作为教堂内部的支撑，用厚实的柱墩支撑拱顶。教堂高耸的钟塔成为朝圣者的定向标志，召唤基督徒在此聚会。教堂建设成为城市的盛事，教堂内外装饰同等重要，美丽雄伟的教堂为城市带来荣耀和自豪。

　　这一时期的教堂和修道院保持了罗马建筑的风格与特征，形成一种教堂建筑风格和装饰艺术风格，称之为罗马式风格或罗马风风格。

5.1 The Later Roman Empire

The Roman Empire reached its greatest territorial extent during the 2nd century. The following two centuries witnessed the slow decline of Roman civilization, including urbanization, population, seaborne commerce, and Roman control over its outlying territories, as the barbarian tribes were growing stronger and pressed in on the borders. So there were many dangers in the empire, even though it was so great and powerful.

In 476 AD, the Western Roman Empire, which had ruled modern-day Italy, France, Spain, Portugal and England for centuries, collapsed due to a combination of economic decline, drastically reduced military strength, and invasion of barbarian tribes.

5.2 The Middle Ages (500–1500 AD)

The "Middle Ages" in European history usually refers to the period from the 5th century to the 15th century, or from the collapse of the Western Roman Empire in 476 to the downfall of Constantinople in 1453, an interim between the ancient world and the modern world. That span from the ancient era to the modern is called the Middle Ages, when Christianity was the dominating force and widely accepted. This period is further subdivided into three stages: the Early Middle Ages, the High Middle Ages and the Late Middle Ages. In fact, the Middle Ages marked the real beginning of European history.

5.3 The Early Middle Ages (500–1000 AD)

The early Middle Ages, from 500 to 1000 AD, is a period featured raiding, migration and conquest of the barbarian tribes. The Western Roman Empire disintegrated into a mosaic of warring kingdoms in the fifth century. There was frequent warfare, decline in the population and virtual disappearance of urban life. Towns and villages fell into ruins and great areas of land lay waste. This period of social collapse was conventionally referred to as "Dark Ages" because of the contrast to the earlier times of Greek and Roman civilizations.

However, out of this period gradually emerged three new civilizations that more or less acquired the cultural heritage of the Classical tradition. In western Europe, the Germanic peoples established new kingdoms that adopted Roman Christianity. In eastern Europe and Asia Minor, the old Roman Empire continued to survive as the Byzantine Empire. As time went by, differences in beliefs and practices arose between the churches in the eastern and western Mediterranean areas. In the 11th century, the Church was divided into the Roman Catholic Church and the Eastern Orthodox Church. The Catholic Church made Latin the official language, while the Eastern Orthodox Church adopted Greek. In western Asia, North Africa and Spain, an Islamic empire emerged and created its own flourishing civilization. Each with its own culture, its own religion, and its own language, these three civilizations quickly became rivals.

The Catholic Church was already a powerful institution at the end of the Roman Empire and it continued to be the unifying force between the many kingdoms, which in a few hundred years would grow into the nations known as England, France, Spain, Italy and Germany. As Roman authority disappeared in the west, cities, literacy, trading networks and urban infrastructure declined. Where civic functions and infrastructure were maintained, it was mainly maintained by the Catholic Church and bishop became a capable civic administrator. The power of the Bishop of Rome expanded and took the title Pope. The Church dominated every aspect of social life.

The church became one of the centers of learning during the Middle Ages. The leading scholars of the early centuries were clergymen for whom the study of nature was pursued more for practical reasons than as an abstract inquiry: the need to care for the sick led to the study of medicine and of ancient texts on drugs, the need for monks to determine the proper time to pray led them to study the motion of the stars, the need to compute the date of Easter led them to study and teach mathematics and the motions of the Sun and Moon. The Church salvaged much from the ruins of the ancient world, selectively preserving some Latin learning, maintaining the art of writing, and preserving a centralized administration through its network of bishops.

After the fall of the Roman Empire, and especially after the expansion of Islam during the seventh century, the monasteries, which sometimes also functioned as cathedrals, were a major source of power in Europe. Bishops and the abbots of important monasteries lived and functioned like princes. Geographically the monasteries were relatively isolated from each other, but as they were based on the same basic values and the same way of life, they were fundamentally similar in structure and organization. As a result, there was a unity to European culture, in spite of political division and poor system of communication.

Down to the eleventh century, the monasteries served as cultural and economic centers and gave rise to the formation of new settlements. For instance, a large village grew up around a monastery, inhabited mostly by craftsmen and their families. The monasteries were also the major institutions of learning of all sorts and that all the arts were to be taught and practiced in the monasteries. Often the only literate members of society were the monks, and few people outside the monasteries could read or write. It was the monks who made and transmitted written copies of the *Bible* and other ancient works from generation to generation. They organized some of the first libraries. Often they conducted scientific and other research to benefit the surrounding communities. They were expert farmers who were able to pass on their expertise to peasants on the large manors. The Hospital of St. John of Jerusalem founded in the 11th century, to care for sick pilgrims, was probably the first organization ever established to offer genuine medical and hospital services. Monasticism played a vital role in the creation, preservation, and transmission of culture.

Life became generally less secure during this period. This resulted in the fortification of many towns, or the rebuilding and strengthening of walls that remained from the Roman period. Many castles were built at strategic points. The enclosure of towns brought about a lack of living space within the walls, and resulted in a style of town house that was tall and narrow, often surrounding communal courtyards. (Fig. 5.1, Fig. 5.2)

Conditions in Western Europe began to improve after 700 AD as Europe experienced an agricultural boom that would continue until at least 1100 AD. Toward the end of this period, Europe experienced a return to systematic agriculture in the form of the feudal system. The basis of feudal society was land and protection. This system featured a hierarchy (kings, lords, knights and villagers) of reciprocal obligations, in which each man was bound to serve his superior in return for the latter's protection. Feudalism played an important role in the preservation of peace and order in society and protection of common people against potential danger, at the same time engaged lords in a series of wars in the process of expanding their territories, thus throwing Europe into a state of disintegration for hundreds of years.

The Early Middle Ages are characterized by the urban control of bishops and the territorial control exercised by noblemen. The rise of urban communes marked the

Chapter Five   The Early Middle Ages   57

Fig. 5.1
Castles were built at strategic points.

Fig. 5.2
Many towns have built city walls.

Fig. 5.3
St. Peter's Basilica was constructed in the 4th century by orders of the Emperor Constantine I. Over the next twelve centuries, the church gradually gained importance, becoming a major place of pilgrimage in Rome.

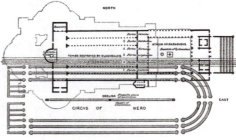

Fig. 5.4
The southern side of Constantine's basilica was erected along the northern side of the Circus Maximus where the ancient Romans held their games. The current basilica was built over the old ruins.

Fig. 5.5
It was constructed in the shape of a cross and consisted of five naves divided by four rows of 22 columns each.

Fig. 5.6
The current basilica was built between 1506 and 1626. The ground plan was a Latin cross. Today, tens of thousands of pilgrims and tourists daily visit the basilica.

beginning of the High Middle Ages.

Pilgrimage

Throughout the Middle Ages, Christians sought to close the distance between themselves and God by engaging in physical travel toward a spiritual goal. The idea of the sacred journey is a feature of many religions, yet by the fourth century AD, pilgrimage had become a recognized expression of Christian piety. Persons from all walks of life made religious journeys, with far-reaching consequences for society and culture as a whole.

The concept and practice of Christian pilgrimage was first made to holy Christian sites which were connected with the birth, life, crucifixion and resurrection of Jesus Christ. The destinations of the first Christian pilgrimages were therefore in the Holy Land, notably Jerusalem—some 3000 miles distant from Europe. Soon it became common for medieval people to make a pilgrimage closer to home visiting sites associated with Christian Saints and martyrs, holy relics. Pilgrimages were the first holidays enjoyed by medieval people. Groups of Christians would set off together on a spiritual journey to visit a holy place where they would pray together. This is the origin of modern travelling.

The city of Rome became another major destination for pilgrims. (Fig. 5.3–Fig. 5.6) Easier of access for European pilgrims than the Holy Land, Rome had also been the home of many saintly martyrs, including Saints Peter and Paul. Constantine erected great basilicas over the tombs of Saints Peter and Paul, and pilgrims visited these as well as other churches associated with miraculous events. A distinction of these sites was the presence of holy relics, material objects like the bones or clothes of the saints, the sight or touch of which was supposed to draw the faithful nearer to saintliness.

Sacred architecture complemented the interior meditations of visitors to the sites of Christ's mission on earth. In the 320s and 330s, Constantine, the first Roman emperor to embrace Christianity, constructed sumptuous buildings on several locations that had already become popular destinations for pilgrims. These churches often incorporated a round or centrally planned element, a form associated with tombs. In Jerusalem, Constantine built a basilica at the place where Christ was crucified and a rotunda around the site of Jesus' burial and resurrection. (Fig. 5.7–Fig. 5.10) In Bethlehem (a Palestinian city, about 10 km south of Jerusalem), Constantine commissioned another church over the cave revered as Jesus' birthplace. The distinctive features of these

Chapter Five   The Early Middle Ages   59

Fig. 5.7 (left)
The entrance of the Church of the Holy Sepulchre

Fig. 5.8 (right)
The rotunda around the site of Jesus' burial and resurrection

Fig. 5.9
Central dome of the Church of the Holy Sepulchre

Fig. 5.10
The dome over Jesus's empty tomb.
The Church of the Holy Sepulchre, also called the Church of the Resurrection in Jerusalem. It contains, according to traditions dating back to at least the fourth century, the two holiest sites in Christianity: the site where Jesus was crucified and Jesus's empty tomb, where he is said to have been buried and resurrected.

Fig. 5.11
A round or centrally planned element, a form associated with tombs. It is also an interior passageway which allowed pilgrims to circulate the relics without interrupting the monks.

buildings were widely copied in churches, tombs, and baptisteries throughout Europe.

Monasteries located along the pilgrimage roads provided food and lodging and also offered prayers. Some monastic churches also housed relics of their own, and these often incorporated an interior passageway called an ambulatory, which allowed pilgrims to circulate and venerate the relics without interrupting the monks in their regular orders of prayer. (Fig. 5.11) The need to accommodate larger numbers of pilgrims caused many churches to undertake major renovations, for example, Saint-Denis, which was dramatically altered in the early twelfth century.

5.4 Romanesque Art and Architecture

Romanesque art is the art of Europe from approximately 1000 AD to the rise of the Gothic style in the 13th century, or later, depending on region. The term was invented by 19th-century art historians, especially for Romanesque architecture, which retained many basic features of Roman architectural style—most notably round-headed arches, barrel vaults, apses, and leaf decoration—but had also developed many different characteristics. Thus Romanesque buildings appeared to be a continuation of the Roman tradition of building.

With the fall of the Roman Empire, the remaining architectural structures of the Western Roman Empire were falling into decay, and Roman building techniques in brick and stone were largely lost in most parts of Europe. But several great basilicas commissioned by Constantine continued to stand as an inspiration to later builders. Where available, Roman brick and stone buildings were recycled for their materials.

Romanesque architecture is known by its massive stone walls, openings topped by semi-circular arches, small windows, sturdy piers (a short section of wall), groin vaults, large towers and decorative arcading. Since massive pillars and walls were required to hold up heavy stone roof, windows were few and small, and the inside of the church was quite dark. Decorative arcading was used to weaken the thickness of the walls. (Fig. 5.12-Fig. 5.14)

As monasticism and pilgrimage spread across Europe, Romanesque churches sprang up and spread in a remarkably similar form, and therefore was the first international style of architecture to come about after the fall of the Roman Empire, prevalent in Europe between 1050-1200. The basic properties of Romanesque architecture stem from a combination of the Early Christian basilica with the protective

Chapter Five   The Early Middle Ages   61

Fig. 5.12
Massive stone walls, openings topped by semi-circular arches, small windows

Fig. 5.13
Florence Baptistery. The two main levels of the structure are ancient, dating probably from the 4th or 5th century, while the uppermost level, pyramidal roof and lantern dates from the 12th century. Many art historians date the beginning of the Italian Renaissance to 1401, the year Lorenzo Ghiberti won the commission to design new east doors for the baptistery.

Fig. 5.14
Since massive pillars and walls were required to hold up heavy stone roof, windows were few and small, and the inside of the church was quite dark.

Fig. 5.15
Senanque Abbey in France.

Fig. 5.16
The organization of some mature Romanesque churches include double aisles, a transept(or two transepts), and the chancel with ambulatory and radiating chapels.

and lofty tower. The organization of a church is a longitudinal basilica, with two towers flanking the entrance and a square tower over the crossing. The organization of some mature Romanesque churches includes double aisles, a transept, and the chancel with ambulatory and radiating chapels. The combination of massive enclosure and large towers is seen as the expression of the desire and the need for assurance and protection. (Fig. 5.16) So the Romanesque church is simultaneously a stronghold and gate to heaven, and is profoundly related with the castle. They are the two main building types of the period.

One of the effects of the Crusade, which was intended to wrest the Holy Places of Palestine from Islamic control, was to excite a great deal of religious fervor, which in turn inspired great building programs.

Despite regional characteristics and different materials, Romanesque was the first style to spread across the whole of Catholic Europe. Large quantity of churches built in the Romanesque period was succeeded by the period of Gothic architecture, which partly or entirely rebuilt most Romanesque churches in prosperous areas. Many Romanesque survivors are in areas that were less prosperous in subsequent periods, including parts of Southern France and Northern Spain. (Fig. 5.15)

The result of the Crusade stimulated further construction of new churches across Europe in the fully fledged Romanesque style. In turn this building program produced a huge demand for decorative religious art, including sculpture, stained glass and other artworks, depicting Christian theme like the Last Judgment and scenes from the Life of Christ. Carvings and sculptured human figures as well as animal forms mentioned in the Bible and ancient fables are often found on windows, doors, capitals, and etc. Bright colors only appeared in stained glass and well-preserved manuscripts. City churches, churches on pilgrimage routes, and many churches in small towns and villages were elaborately decorated.

New Words and Expressions

seaborne　　*a.* 经由海上（运输）的
outlying　　*a.* 边远的；偏远的；远离市镇的
drastic　　*a.* 急剧地；猛烈地
interim　　*n.* 期间；间歇

raid　*n.* 突袭
clergyman　*n.* 神职人员中的一员
Easter　*n.* 复活节
salvage　*vt.* 挽救
abbot　*n.* 男修道院院长
manor　*n.* 庄园
pilgrim　*n.* 朝圣者
fortification　*n.* 防御工事
communal　*a.* 公共的
hierarchy　*n.* 等级制度
lord　*n.* 庄园主；封建主
reciprocal　*a.* 互惠的；相互的
obligation　*n.* （法律、责任、合同等）义务
disintegration　*n.* 分裂；分解
commune　*n.* 群体；公社
piety　*n.* 虔诚
crucifixion　*n.* 受难
resurrection　*n.* 复活
saint　*n.* ［缩略 St. or S］（教会正式尊崇的）圣徒
martyr　*n.* 殉道者
miraculous　*a.* 神奇的
relic　*n.* 圣徒遗物；圣物；圣骨；遗迹；遗物
complement　*vt.* 完善；补充
meditation　*n.* 调解；调停；斡旋
sumptuous　*a.* 豪华的；奢华的
incorporate　*vt.* 把……并入；吸收；包含
rotunda　*n.* 圆形建筑（尤指拱顶的）；圆形大厅
Bethlehem　伯利恒（巴勒斯坦中部城市。根据《圣经》记载，伯利恒是耶稣的出生地）
revere　*vt.* 尊敬；敬畏
baptistery　*n.* 洗礼堂
ambulatory　*n.* （教堂）回廊
venerate　*vt.* 尊重；敬重
renovation　*n.* 修复；更新

Romanesque   *n.* 罗马式；罗曼式；罗马风
Gothic   *n.* 哥特风格
round-headed arch   *n.* 圆形拱
barrel vault   *n.* 桶形穹顶
semi-circular arch   *n.* 半圆拱
pier   *n.* 柱墩；墙墩；桥墩
groin vault   *n.* 交叉穹顶；十字穹顶 (the sharp curved edge made by the intersection of vaults crossing each other)
chapel   *n.* （教堂内的）小礼拜堂
stronghold   *n.* 堡垒；要塞；据点
Crusade   *n.* 十字军东征
wrest   *vt.* 夺下；抢去
fledge   *a.* 成熟的；独立的
stained glass   *n.* 彩色玻璃
manuscript   *n.* 手稿

Chapter Six Islamic Culture

导读

公元 7 世纪,穆罕默德创立了伊斯兰教,随后,一个强大的阿拉伯帝国崛起,横跨亚非欧。

对于伊斯兰世界来说,中世纪是伊斯兰文明发展的黄金时代,其文化和商业得到空前发展,学术和技术在西欧处于领先地位,这些成就为 14 世纪的欧洲文艺复兴奠定了基础。所有这一切都源自伊斯兰世界的开放包容,大量吸收了其广阔疆域中的基督教文化、犹太文化、罗马文化、希腊文化和印度等地区的文化。

这一时期,穆斯林世界成为全球科学与文化教育的中心,公共性质的医院、图书馆、大学等机构首先在这里出现。早期的科学研究方法在这里形成,实证、实验和定量分析的方法被用于科学探究。穆斯林对医学的贡献也是巨大的,古希腊的医学得到进一步研究与应用,其治疗方法被十字军带回欧洲,改善了欧洲的医疗状况。大量古希腊经典著作被译成阿拉伯文得以保存,这些著作后来经西班牙和西西里岛传播到西方世界。

随着伊斯兰文明的发展,一种广泛运用于清真寺和装饰品的伊斯兰建筑与艺术在伊比利亚半岛和北非地区形成,被称为摩尔建筑与艺术。其主要表现形式为广泛应用拱券(尖拱、马蹄拱、花瓣形拱等)和穹隆等建筑结构的装饰体系,用复杂的几何图形、植物花卉纹样和伊斯兰经文装饰墙面、门洞和窗孔。

6.1 Muslim Conquest (632–750 AD)

In the 7th century Islam was founded by Muhammad (born in Mecca, 570–632) in Arabia. An Islamic empire was established shortly afterwards and soon conquered the Middle East, North Africa, Spain, central Asia, and India. (Fig. 6.1) The Arab Empire expanded explosively and eroded the area of Roman Empire, controlled strategic areas of the Mediterranean Sea. In the east it attacked Constantinople; in the west it invaded

Chapter Six   Islamic culture   67

Fig. 6.1
The Arab Empire soon conquered the Middle East, North Africa, Spain, central Asia, and India.

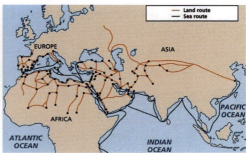

Fig. 6.2
Arab trade networks extend from the Atlantic Ocean and Mediterranean Sea in the west to the Indian Ocean and China Sea in the east.

Spain and then France. By the early eighth century, Iberia and Sicily had fallen to the Muslims. Only in 732 was the Muslim advance into Europe stopped. However, the Islamic conquests permanently removed all of North Africa from the Western world.

In the early 1200s, a powerful Mongol Empire emerged in central Asia. By 1260, most of the Islamic east was under Mongol control and the Arab Empire was gone.

6.2 The Flourish of Islamic Culture

Literally, Islam means "devotion to God," more specifically to Allah, the One God. Those who practice such devotion and submit themselves to the will of Allah (the Arabic word for God) are Muslims. This belief in the One God and in Muhammad as his Prophet unites Muslims throughout the world.

Within the bond of a common religion, many distinctive local, cultural and ethnic features developed quite early, since Islam constantly absorbed elements of the cultures it had conquered or converted. To that extent, Islam may be described as "diversity within unity." Islamic culture is a combination of unity and variety, giving it a prominent position among the religions and cultures of the world.

In the Islamic World, the Middle Ages is known as the Islamic Golden Age of learning, commerce, and civilization. Many ideas that came out of Islamic lands laid the foundation for the European Renaissance in the 1400s. During the early Middle Ages and the Islamic Golden Age (from the 8th to 13th centuries A.D), Islamic philosophy, science, and technology were more advanced than in Western Europe. However, much of Islamic learning and science were not Arabian in origin; in fact, they were influenced by the people the Muslims conquered. Jews, Christians, Hindus, Greeks, Persians and Africans all contributed to the development of Islamic culture. Islamic scholars both preserved and built upon earlier Ancient Greek and Roman traditions and also added their own inventions and innovations.

One reason the Islamic world flourished was religious freedom. Though the empire was ruled by the laws based on the messages Muhammad received from Allah, people throughout the empire modeled their behavior on the moral teachings and examples set by Muhammad. Tolerance to other faiths helped create cross-cultural networks by attracting Muslim, Christian and Jewish intellectuals to study and translate the world's knowledge into Arabic. Here the Muslim world was a furnace of cultures which collected, synthesized and significantly advanced the knowledge gained from the ancient Mesopotamian, Roman, Chinese, Indian, Persian, Egyptian, North African, Greek and Byzantine civilizations.

During this period the Muslim world became the unrivaled intellectual center for science, philosophy, medicine and education. In Muslim cities, knowledge and learning were nurtured and encouraged. Scholars throughout the empire learned about science and philosophy by reading the works of the ancient Greeks, which were all translated into Arabic, as ancient Greek was not a widely known language. The first people to translate these works were mainly Jews and Christians in Syria. Thanks to the Arabic translations of the Greek masters, preserved in vast libraries throughout the Arab Empire, Europe was eventually exposed to those important works of mathematics, astronomy, and logic. It was from Spain and Sicily that these translations eventually made their way into the Western world, where they were translated into Latin.

To facilitate translation and learning, the Muslims established the "House of Wisdom" in Baghdad, which included a library, a translation bureau, and a school. Many classic works of antiquity that would otherwise have been forgotten were translated into Arabic. Baghdad was the center of Muslim thought and rule, and then expanded slowly and eventually nearly everywhere in the region.

Another common feature during the Islamic Golden Age was the large number of Muslim scholars, each of whom contributed to a variety of different fields of both religious and secular learning. Many medieval Muslim thinkers pursued humanistic, rational and scientific discourses in their search for knowledge, meaning and values. Early scientific methods were developed in the Islamic world, where an empirical, experimental and quantitative approach to scientific inquiry was adopted.

Among the most important Islamic contributions were their advances in the field of medicine. By applying and adding to Greek medical theory, the physicians of the empire were the most advanced of their time. European Crusaders brought home some of their treatments, which helped advance European medical practices. Europeans benefited most from the innovation of Arabic numerals, which freed mathematicians from the use of the awkward Roman numbers. The concept of zero was also introduced by the Arabs. Both Arabic mathematics and numerals laid down the foundation of modern mathematics in the West.

A number of important educational and scientific institutions previously unknown in the ancient world have their origins in the early Islamic world, with the most notable examples such as the public hospital and psychiatric hospital, the public library, the academic degree-granting university. There was also an observatory from which scholars and scientists could study the stars and planets. Arabic translations of Greek works, along with Islamic advances in learning, laid foundation for modern science, medicine and other fields of learning.

6.2.1 Pilgrimage and Trade

The tradition of the pilgrimage to Mecca makes it a center for exchanging ideas and goods. Before Muhammad, Arabian tribes practiced a type of worship that attributes supernatural powers to objects in nature, such as stones. Mecca is not only the direction of prayer for Muslims wherever they are, but is also the place to which all Muslims must go as pilgrims at least once in their lifetime. Each year, thousands of pilgrims made their way to Mecca to take part in religious festivals centered round the Kaaba, a large cube-shaped structure made of dark stone, in the center of town. As an important stop along many caravan routes between Syria, Iraq, Southwestern Arabia, and the Red Sea, Mecca was not only a trade center in Arabia but also the center of religion for most Arabs.

The influence held by Muslim merchants over trade routes was tremendous. Merchants brought goods and their faith to China, India, South-east Asia and North Africa and returned with new inventions. As a result, Islamic civilization grew and expanded on the basis of its merchant economy. An early global economy was established across most of Asia and Africa and much of Europe, with their trade networks extending from the Atlantic Ocean and Mediterranean Sea in the west to the Indian Ocean and China Sea in the east. This helped establish the Islamic Empire as the world's leading extensive economic power throughout the 7th–13th centuries.

With the introduction of papermaking, there were hundreds of shops specializing in books in Baghdad, and even public libraries began to become established. From here paper-making spread west to Europe in the 13th century.

Owing to the influence of Islamic culture and civilization in Islamic Spain and southern Italy, and in the eastern part of the Mediterranean Sea, Western Europeans translated many Arabic texts into Latin during the Middle Ages. Islamic Spain passed much of the Muslim achievements on to Europe.

6.2.2 Urbanization

Muslims were great city builders. Baghdad was the largest and most cultured city in the Middle East by the early 800s. At its height, more than 1 million people made their homes there. It contained breathtaking mosques, palaces, and gardens. It was also home to libraries, colleges, and hospitals, attracting people from all over the world to study and do business there.

As urbanization increased, Muslim cities grew unregulated, resulting in narrow winding city streets and neighborhoods separated by different ethnic and religious backgrounds. These qualities proved efficient for transporting goods to and from major commercial centers while preserving the privacy valued by Islamic family life.

Muslim cities also had advanced domestic water systems with sewers, public baths, drinking fountains, piped drinking water supplies, and widespread private and public toilet and bathing facilities. The average lifespan in the lands under Islamic rule was much longer than that of Greco-Roman world, due to the agricultural progress as well as improved medical care.

6.3 Muslim Influence in Spain

Muslim Spain was the gem of Europe. The Arabs, unlike other invaders in Europe in the Dark Age, brought a high degree of civilization with them. Their religion, science and urban way of life were well expressed in the capital city of Islamic Spain, Cordoba,

Fig. 6.3
Moorish decorative patterns and tile

Fig. 6.4
Calligraphy used for decoration

a former Roman city. Reaching a population of half a million, it became the largest and most prosperous city in Western Europe, while London was a tiny mud-hut village at the time.

Cordoba was not only a center of trade and industry in the area, but also a center of learning and culture, not only for the Muslim world but for Europe as well. From Cordoba and other cities in Spain, poetry, science, philosophy, and medical knowledge spread throughout the Islamic Empire and into Europe. Many important goods were introduced to Europe via Muslim Spain. One of Muslim Spain's key contributions to Europe was the introduction of paper. The production of paper spread from China to the Middle East, and then to Spain, Italy, and the rest of Europe. Paper-making enabled people to produce books more cheaply, and encouraged the spread of learning and knowledge throughout Europe.

6.4. Moorish Art and Architecture

With the conquest of most of Spain by Muslim Arabs in the eighth century, an architecture which has no parallel in Europe emerged. Moorish art and architecture is a branch of Islamic art and architecture developed in the westernmost lands of the Muslims. It is a term used to describe the articulated Islamic architecture which developed in North Africa and south-western Europe, especially the Iberian Peninsula.

As Islam spread, a distinctive style of Islamic art gradually developed. It was used mainly for religious architecture, book illustrations, and the decoration of objects. Historically, Islamic art was influenced by the artistic styles of the conquered regions. It has developed from a wide variety of different sources, which include elements from Greek, Roman, and early Christian art which it combines with the great Middle Eastern cultures of Egypt, Byzantium, and ancient Persia.

The development of Islamic art was also influenced by two religious restrictions. Mohammed warned artists not to imitate God, by making images of living things. Most religious art therefore consisted of ornamental designs that did not represent people or animals. The restriction on making images led to the development of one of the most outstanding features of Islamic art. Artists developed a special kind of decoration—a very complicated design. It can consist of twisting patterns of plants and flowers. It can be made up of geometric shapes and patterns of straight lines, or it can have curving lines that twist and turn over each other. Sometimes animal shapes were used, but they were always highly stylized and not lifelike. (Fig. 6.3)

The second restriction discouraged the use of costly materials. Therefore, Islamic artists learned to decorate objects made of less expensive materials so skillfully that they looked as beautiful as silver or gold.

Another important characteristic of Islamic art is the use of calligraphy, or beautiful handwriting. Arabic can be beautifully written in several different kinds of script. Islamic artists used Arabic script as part of their designs for religious books, wall decorations, and art objects. Especially beautiful calligraphy and decoration were used for copies of the Koran, the holy book of the Islamic faith. (Fig. 6.4)

The most architectural achievement of the Islamic Empire was the mosque, which served as a place of worship, the heart of a community, a court of justice, etc. A mosque is permanently and appropriately associated with the presence of Islam. Technically it

Chapter Six Islamic culture   73

Fig. 6.5
The Dome of the Rock in Jerusalem
The oldest mosque in Jerusalem adopted the octagonal plan of early Christian church. Under the dome in the center is the rock which is believed to be the place from where the Prophet Muhammed ascended to heaven during his night journey to Jerusalem.

Fig. 6.6
Mosaic decoration

Fig. 6.7
San Lorenzo, Milan, early Christian church

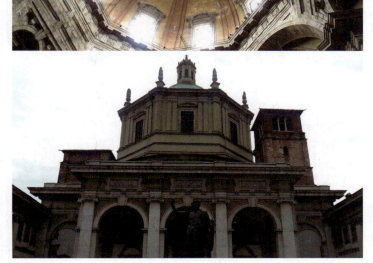

Fig. 6.8
Centralized plan, octagonal dome

74　An Introduction to Western Culture and Art

Fig. 6.9
The Cathedral standing exactly in the Mosque's center
The great mosque falls into two parts, the courtyard to the north and the huge prayer hall, which comprises 19 aisles (composed of rows of colonnades) running from the east to west, each with a saddleback roof（鞍形屋顶）. Within the mosque's center lies the massive cathedral structure, begun in the 16th century and completed in the 18th century. The freestanding former mosque tower now functions as the cathedral's bell tower. The southern exterior wall faces Mecca.

means the place where believers conduct prayer, the main action required every day of all Muslims in order to express their faith. What is implied here is not a specific and new kind of building, something which did not really exist at the time of the Prophet, but a space reserved for the community of believers in which they can gather to pray, and to deal with communal affairs. With the conquest of so many different lands where Muslims had to find or build their own restricted spaces, mosque emerged as a separate and individualized building with an architectural typology of its own and a set of technical requirements peculiar to it.

　　Some of the early mosques were former Christian churches, as no Islamic building tradition existed yet. The first mosques were designed and built by architects and craftsmen from around the empire and they incorporated some of the stylistic

Chapter Six　Islamic culture　　75

Fig. 6.10
Aisles composed of rows of colonnades in the huge prayer hall

Fig. 6.11
Interior of the Cathedral

Fig. 6.12
The Alhambra Palace

Fig. 6.13
Ground plan

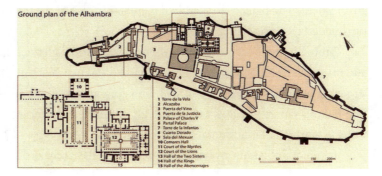

elements from their region into the mosque's structure and design. For example, the dome of Byzantine Empire was used in designing some mosques. The early prototype for the mosque included a columned hall oriented toward Mecca, the holy city of Islam, and an adjacent courtyard surrounded by a colonnade. All Muslims face in the direction of Mecca when they pray. The oldest existing mosque, the Dome of the Rock in Jerusalem, was built in 691. It has many features of Byzantine Christian churches, including a large central dome, columns and mosaic decorations. (Fig. 6.5-Fig. 6.8)

The Spanish Muslims began construction of the dominant building in Cordoba, the Great Mosque, in 785 marking the beginning of Islamic architecture in Spain and Northern Africa. The mosque, built on the site occupied by a Christian church, is noted for its striking interior arches. (Fig. 6.9)

The Great Mosque comprises a rectangular prayer hall, with a courtyard in front. The courtyard is nearly as large as the prayer hall, where originally believers also assembled for prayers if the hall was already full. The prayer hall is like an enlarged version of an ancient Roman basilica combined with a forest of columns, which formed eleven aisles. The center aisle, wider and higher than all the other ones, serves as the central axis, leading to the prayer niche, and indicating the direction of prayers to Mecca. During the 10th century, the mosque was extended southwards with eight side aisles added, far larger than the courtyard. (Fig. 6.10, Fig. 6.11)

In the 16th century, the cathedral regained the mosque territory. Accordingly, 63 columns were removed from the mosque, so that the cathedral could stand exactly in the mosque's center.

The second to mosques were royal palaces with pools, gardens and fountains in the courtyard. Standing on a high plateau, the Alhambra kept watching over the capital city situated at its feet, and acted as the administrative and power center of Granada. This typical Islamic palace complex contains the ruler's residence and seat of government. The palaces looked like Roman fortresses, for they were built of stone and surrounded by walls with big towers.

Moorish architecture reached its peak with the construction of the Alhambra, the magnificent palace/fortress of Granada. The Palace, built in the 14th century, is the largest Islamic fortress in Spain, with amazing architectural details and a large garden. The famous Court of Lions features over 120 intricately carved white marble columns, and a beautiful 12-lion fountain in its center. (Fig. 6.12-Fig. 6.17)

Islamic architecture was distinguished by the arches, domes, traceried windows,

Chapter Six   Islamic culture   77

**Fig. 6.14
Fountains, gardens and secluded courtyards**

**Fig. 6.15
Court of Lions**

**Fig. 6.16 (left)
Wall decoration**

**Fig. 6.17 (right)
Dome**

decorative tile work, decorative script or patterns, fountains, gardens and secluded courtyards. Many different arts were used in the decoration of Islamic mosques and palaces. The basic components of Islamic ornament are calligraphy, vegetal patterns and geometric patterns. Islamic calligraphy is associated with geometric Islamic art on the walls and ceilings of mosques and palaces as well as on the page. The Muslims also adopted the art forms of conquered peoples, particularly the use of decorative mosaics.

New Words and Expressions

Muhammad 穆罕默德
Arabia 阿拉伯；阿拉伯半岛
erode *vt.* 侵蚀；腐蚀
Iberia *n.* 伊比利亚；伊比利亚半岛
Mongol *n.* 蒙古人
prophet *n.* （基督教、犹太教、伊斯兰教的）先知
furnace *n.* 熔炉
synthesize *vt.* 综合；使合成
nurture *vt.* 发展；培养
secular *a.* 非宗教的；世俗的
observatory *n.* 天文台；观象台
gem *n.* 宝石；珠宝；精品
cube-shaped *a.* 立方造型的
caravan *n.* （尤指往返于沙漠地带的）旅行队
Greco-Roman *a.* 希腊罗马的
articulated *a.* 链接的；连接的
Moorish *a.* 摩尔人的；摩尔文化的
Koran *n.* 可兰经
adjacent *a.* 邻近的
intricate *a.* 错综复杂的
traceried *a.* 线条交错的美丽图案
secluded *a.* 僻静的；偏僻的；隐居的

Chapter Seven　Byzantine Culture

导读

　　当西罗马帝国渐渐走向衰败与灭亡时，东罗马帝国奇迹般地得以延续并走向辉煌，史称拜占庭帝国。拜占庭帝国不仅保留了古希腊罗马文化，还吸收了阿拉伯伊斯兰文化，在此基础上发展了拜占庭文化艺术和科学技术，并将其传播到欧洲。帝国的都城君士坦丁堡也依照罗马的规模进行了大规模的修建。

　　从时间顺序上看，拜占庭建筑艺术是与早期基督教建筑艺术同时期发展起来的，拜占庭建筑艺术是罗马建筑艺术的延续，以早期基督教的集中式教堂为基础，平面呈圆形、八角形或十字形，上方覆盖穹顶。成熟的拜占庭风格教堂多采用十字型，其四翼上各有一个穹顶或半穹顶承托和拱卫位于中央的穹顶，外观上看似一个穹顶的迷阵。教堂内部多采用马赛克镶嵌艺术装饰。

7.1 Byzantine Empire (330–1453 AD)

As the Western Roman Empire weakened and vanished in the 5th century, the richer Eastern Roman Empire managed to survive and to recover its strength. It continued through the Middle Ages and to the beginning of the Modern Era. The collapse of the Western Roman Empire made the Eastern Roman Empire, conventionally referred to as Byzantine Empire, the legal successor to the classical Roman Empire. However, Byzantine Empire had little ability to assert control over the lost western territories.

When Emperor Constantine moved the capital of the Roman Empire to Constantinople in 330 AD, his intention was to mark the beginning of a new era. Constantinople looked at Rome as an archetype, brought many things to greater perfection and splendor. In 1411, Byzantine scholar Manuel Chrysoloras was sent to Rome on a diplomatic mission by the emperor. He wrote an extended comparison between the city of Rome and Constantinople, the capital of the Byzantine Empire: "I think that our city is superior for many things were made, and still exist, in Constantinople, that Rome does not have."

The location of the new capital is significant. It was set where Asia and Europe meet. Not only do the continents of the East and the West meet here, the Black Sea and the Mediterranean are also connected, forming an intersection, where the city of Constantinople seems to be hovering between heaven and earth. Approaching from the sea, the city skyline was dominated by the innumerable "heavenly" domes of churches. Over them all rose Hagia Sophia. By the early eighth century, Constantinople was one of the largest and wealthiest cities of the entire world. Greek replaced Latin as the official language of the Empire.

7.2 Byzantine Architecture and Art

Early Byzantine architecture was simply a continuation of Roman architecture. Two major types of churches can be distinguished: the basilica type, with a nave flanked by colonnades terminating in a semicircular apse and covered by a timber roof; (Fig. 4.8, Fig. 4.9) the stone-vaulted centralized church, with its separate components gathered under a central dome. (Fig. 4.11, Fig. 6.7, Fig. 6.8) The second type, the stone-vaulted centralized church was dominant throughout the Byzantine period.

The centralized plan was adopted for the major churches. This pattern became the distinguishing property of Byzantine church architecture from the 5th century. The early churches based on the domed and octagonal plan, or a simple cross-domed plan, where a dome surmounts the crossing of nave and transept. In larger structures, five domed units were arranged to form a Greek cross. (Fig. 7.1) In later Byzantine architecture the cross-domed church developed into the standard cross-in-square church, where the corners are surmounted by smaller domes, and the chancel is accompanied by smaller apses on either side. This array of domes roofed greater interior space.

The centralized space of the Byzantine church is covered by a dome, representing heaven. Divine light emanated from the heavenly dome and spread to the centralized space below. (Fig. 7.2)

The largest and the most technically advanced edifice of Byzatine architecture was the Hagia Sophia, built in the 6th century. The vast interior has a complex structure. The nave is covered by a central dome. At the western and eastern side, there

Chapter Seven Byzantine Culture

Fig. 7.1
St Mark's Basilica. Five domed units were arranged to form a Greek cross. The chancel is accompanied by smaller apses on either side.

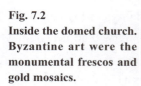

Fig. 7.2
Inside the domed church. Byzantine art were the monumental frescos and gold mosaics.

are arched openings extended by half domes of identical diameter to the central dome, carried on smaller semi-domes; a hierarchy of dome-headed elements built up to create a vast oblong interior crowned by the central dome. (Fig. 7.3–Fig. 7.6)

Its interior is decorated with mosaics and marble pillars and coverings of great artistic value. The main achievements of Byzantine art were the monumental frescos and mosaics inside domed churches, most of which have not survived due to natural disasters and the appropriation of the church to mosque.

The building was later converted into an Ottoman mosque in the 1450s, with four towers added. It was then secularized and opened as a museum in 1935.

The domed churches of Constantinople and Eastern Europe were to greatly affect the architecture of certain towns, particularly through trade and through the Crusade. The most notable single building which demonstrates this is St Mark's Basilica, Venice and there are many less known examples, particularly in France.

7.3 Other Achievements

Byzantine scholars played an important role in the transmission of classical knowledge to the Islamic world and to Renaissance Italy, and also in the transmission of medieval Arabic knowledge to Renaissance Italy. Its rich historiographical tradition preserved ancient knowledge upon which splendid art, architecture, literature and technological achievements were built. Byzantine's another great intellectual achievement was the "Body of Civil Law", a massive compilation of Roman law.

Byzantine scientists preserved and continued the legacy of the great Ancient Greek mathematicians and put mathematics in practice. In the Early Middle Ages, Byzantine architects and mathematicians used complex mathematical formulas to construct the great Hagia Sophia temple, a magnificent technological breakthrough for its time and for centuries afterwards due to its striking geometry, bold design and height.

The Eastern Roman Empire, comprising Greece, the Balkans, Asia Minor, Syria and Egypt, was under strong Greek cultural influence. Despite the later loss of Syria and Egypt to the Arab Empire, the Eastern Roman Empire lived on for another millennium, until its last remains were finally annexed by the emerging Turkish Ottoman Empire.

Chapter Seven   Byzantine Culture   83

Fig. 7.3
Hagia Sophia

Fig. 7.4
Divine light emanated from the heavenly dome and spread to the centralized space below.

Fig. 7.5 (left)
Ground plan of centralized church

Fig. 7.6 (right)
The vaulting of the nave

New Words and Expressions

successor　　*n.* 继承者
archetype　　*n.* 原型；典型
intersection　　*n.* 交叉口；交点
terminate　　*vi. & vt.* 结束；终止
stone-vaulted　　*a.* 石拱的（an architectural term for an arched form used to provide a space with a ceiling or roof）
cross-domed　　*a.* 十字圆顶形的（A cross-in-square or crossed-dome plan features a square center with an internal structure shaped like a cross, topped by a dome）
cross-in-square　　*n.* 十字平面形
surmount　　*vi. & vt.* 居于……之上；在……顶上
emanate　　*vi.* 来自；散发自
oblong　　*n. & a.* 椭圆形；长方形
appropriation　　*n.* 擅用；私占
secularize　　*vt.* 改作俗用；使还俗
historiographical　　*a.* 编史的；史料编纂的
compilation　　*n.* 编辑；编纂

Chapter Eight   The High and Late Middle Ages

导读

  中世纪鼎盛期见证了欧洲城市化的进程、现代民族国家的兴起和意大利城邦的繁荣兴盛，商业行会随之形成，专业性的贸易集市和展会定期举行，现代意义上的大学开始出现。

  教堂成为城市建设的主题，教堂不仅是市民的精神依托，更是城市荣耀、经济繁荣、工艺精湛的具体体现。为了减轻教堂穹顶的压力，结构上采用尖拱券作为连续的穹顶，外侧以飞扶壁为依托，避免了罗马式半圆拱产生的强大侧推力，从而，原本罗马式厚重压抑的石墙被纤细的石柱与巨大彩色玻璃窗构成的通透的框架构筑所取代，自然光穿过彩色玻璃变得神圣迷离。向上生长的列柱使教堂的高度戏剧般地上升，尖拱形成的韵律创造出神秘的精神空间。哥特风格随之形成。

  除了教堂，哥特风格还被广泛应用于城堡、宫殿、市政厅、行会大厦和大学建筑。

8.1 The High Middle Ages (1000–1300 AD)

  The High Middle Ages were characterized by the urbanization of Europe, military expansion, and intellectual revival between the 11th century and the end of the 13th century. This age witnessed an explosion in population, which flowed into towns, the rise of modern nation-states in Western Europe and the growth of the great Italian city-states. The cities of antiquity had been clustered around the Mediterranean. By 1200, the growing urban centers were in the centre of the continent, connected by roads or rivers. (Fig. 8.1) At the end of this period, Paris might have had as many as 200,000 inhabitants. In central and northern Italy, the rise of towns that were self-governing to some degree within their territories stimulated the economy and created an environment for new types of religious and trade associations—guilds. And some Italian city-states such as Venice, Genoa, and Pisa expanded their trade throughout the Mediterranean.

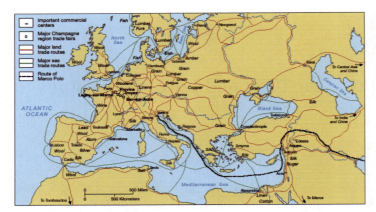

Fig. 8.1
The towns were connected by a network of roads

The High Middle Ages also produced many different forms of intellectual, spiritual and artistic works. The still-powerful Roman Church called for a series of religious wars known as the Crusade.

8.1.1 Pilgrimage (11th–12th Century)

With the growing importance to worship the relics of certain saints, some places gained particular importance and were visited by large numbers of pilgrims. The most important pilgrimage destination in Europe was the church of St. James at Santiago de Compostela in Spain, which, with Jerusalem and Rome, was one of the three most sacred places to visit. During the eleventh century the roads to Santiago from France became grand routes of communication. (Fig. 8.2) On each of the routes monasteries were established to cater for the flow of people and grew wealthy from the passing trade. With the pilgrimage roads connecting several important ecclesiastical centers, the Church was on its way to giving Europe a common cultural basis.

Rome was particularly rich in relics, but as the Middle Ages progressed, other places acquired important relics and became centers of pilgrimage themselves. In the eleventh and twelfth centuries, huge numbers of pilgrims flocked to Santiago de Compostela in northern Spain, where the relics of Saint James the Greater were believed to have been discovered around 830 AD. Canterbury was a popular destination for English pilgrims, who traveled to witness the relics of Thomas Becket, the sainted archbishop of Canterbury.

Fig. 8.2
The roads to Santiago from France became grand routes of communication.

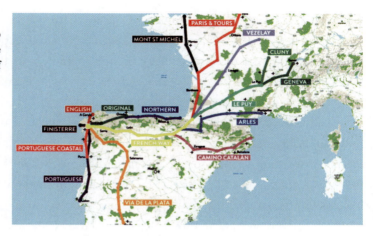

Fig. 8.3
The Crusade routes

8.1.2 The Crusade

As previously stated the first Christian pilgrimages were made to the Holy Land, a massive undertaking carried out by thousands of people. But in 1065 Jerusalem was taken by the Islamic Turks, which made the Medieval Christian community horrified. They believed that it was a sacred undertaking to make a pilgrimage to Jerusalem and this conviction changed the pilgrimage into a military campaign.

The Crusade (1095–1270) were armed pilgrimages intended to retake the Holy Land, particularly Jerusalem, from the Muslims that had conquered it from the Christian Byzantine Empire during a rapid military expansion in the 7th century. One consequence was that the Latin-speaking world regained access to the civilization of Byzantine, with all its great learning and much treasure; the Mediterranean Sea was reopened to Christian shipping and the northern coastal towns. (Fig. 8.3) One unanticipated byproduct of the Crusade was to facilitate the spread of Islamic goods, culture, and thought to Europe. They brought home goods that soon became very popular, including spices, foods, and textiles. However, deeper distrust was created between Islam and Christianity.

The Crusade brought about a very large movement of people and, with them, ideas and trade skills, particularly those involved in the building of fortifications and the metal working needed for the provision of arms, which was also applied to the fitting and decoration of buildings. The continual movement of people, rulers, nobles, bishops, craftsmen and peasants, was an important factor in creating a similarity in building methods and a recognizable Romanesque style, despite regional differences.

8.1.3 Medieval Towns

During this period, the urban settlement regained its basic importance. From the 11th century on, a general process of urbanization took place in Western and Central Europe as a result of a considerable growth in population. Old centers from Roman times regained the vitality, small villages developed into towns, and innumerable new settlements were founded. Some of them became regional centers, usually because of an interaction of cultural (religious) and economic factors. The process first took place in Italy and then spread to France, where a particularly dense concentration of medieval towns occurred. The towns were connected by a network of roads, with one day's journey as the standard distance. However, communication was easy only in summer, and medieval towns could be regarded as relatively isolated self-sufficient units.

Towns arose because of trade, but they also stimulated trade by providing greater markets and by producing goods for the merchants to sell. Rivers were also important in the development of medieval towns. They were natural highways on which articles of commerce could be easily transported.

Although the towns of the later Middle Ages appear irregular and picturesque, they all conform to a pattern of narrow streets, having near the center a market square, a church and a town hall. (Fig. 8.4) Nearly all were fortified with impressive walls. Regardless of size, they had basic properties in common: enclosure, density, intimacy, and functional differentiation. The functional differentiation involved the specialization of streets and quarters for certain purposes, such as types of handicraft and profession. This pattern reflected the fact that merchants and craftsman were organized into guilds, which were both religious clubs and trade associations. Merchant guilds were established for the sake of companionship and protection as well as for the purpose of extending and regulating trade. Craft guilds were concerned with the maintenance of standards of craftsmanship and with the development of a system of training by apprenticeship. Because the guild was so involved in every aspect of the craft and trade, members often formed a very tight community in one area of a town or city.

The city wall was of particular importance in that it offered the necessary protection to make the town function as a "container", as well as a "magnet", where a true communal life could develop and a pride of citizenship arose. In this sense, the medieval town resembles a living organism, where the wall is the hard shell and the church the delicate core, with the dwellings spread in between. In addition, the city wall was a symbol of a domain reigned by law, order and security. The medieval town is something more than a physical enclosure; it creates a feeling of being "inside", or being "somewhere", which is lost in the modern town.

Some towns gained their independence by paying lords to grant it to them, while others governed alongside their lord. Still others battled violently for rights of self-governance. Many towns in Italy were particularly successful. They gained the right not only to govern themselves but also to rule the farmland and villages around them. By the 13th century, northern Italy was divided politically and economically into competing city-states, regions dominated by their chief city. In many places, the town hall in the city center served as an expression of the freedom of the burghers.

8.1.4 Fairs

Fairs were important and elaborate events held either seasonally or annually in specified areas in medieval towns. They were the most colorful events in towns and cities. Merchants in different towns traded with one another at great markets or fairs. Fairs were markets and festivals rolled into one. They attracted foreign merchants and traders who bought and sold luxuries and exchanged a great deal of money. Kings, dukes, and other princes sponsored fairs, providing protection for the merchants and assigning them places to stay in town. They reduced normal taxes and tolls, and in return they took a percentage of the profits. Fairs were important sources of income for their sponsors. Fairs usually took place during church festivals, and sometimes they were even set up on church grounds. Fairs also greatly stimulated the revival of a money economy and early forms of banking and credit.

Fig. 8.4
Palazzo Pubblico. Civic building was of great importance to medieval towns as a sign of wealth and pride.

Fig. 8.5
Milan Cathedral. Architecture, sculpture and painting were unified in the creation of church building.

Fig. 8.6
The central nave

8.2 Gothic Architecture and Art

Gothic architecture is a style of medieval architecture that developed out of Romanesque style and flourished during the high and late medieval period. Originating in 12th-century France and lasting into the 16th century, Gothic architecture was the architecture of many churches, abbeys, castles, palaces, town halls, guild halls, and universities of Europe. It was in the great churches and in a number of civic buildings that the Gothic style was expressed most powerfully.

The earliest Gothic art was monumental sculpture, on the walls of Cathedrals and abbeys. Secular art came into its own during this period with the rise of cities, foundation of universities, increase in trade, the establishment of a money-based economy and the creation of a bourgeois class who could afford to patronize the arts and commission works resulting in a proliferation of paintings and illuminated manuscripts.

For those flourishing towns that grew in comparative peace, in trade and competition with each other or united for mutual wealth, civic building was of great importance as a sign of wealth and pride. The construction of cathedral became the leading building task. It was physically in the heart of the city and mentally in the hearts of the citizens. It was the chief building in the village and in the city, and represented in its workmanship the enduring faith of the people. To achieve this end, architecture, sculpture and painting were unified in the creation of church building. (Fig. 8.5–Fig. 8.7)

Gothic architecture first appeared when the abbey church of St. Denis in France was rebuilt in 1140. The plan of the cathedral is based on the organization of the major churches of mature Romanesque architecture, manifesting the fundamental themes of longitudinality and centralization. But the nave became relatively shorter, the projection of the transept less evident, and the chancel larger.

The characteristic features of Gothic architecture include the pointed arch, the ribbed vault and the flying buttress. The ribbed vault, unlike the semi-circular vault of Roman and Romanesque buildings, was much lighter and more elegant than the cross vault characteristic of the Romanesque. It can be used to roof rectangular and irregularly shaped plans. Another structural advantage is that the pointed arch channels the weight onto the much thinner bearing piers or columns at a steep angle.

Fig. 8.7
Pointed arch and sculpture

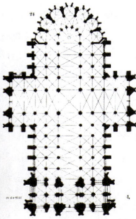

Fig. 8.8
Cologne Cathedral. The plan of Gothic cathedral is based on the organization of mature Romanesque architecture. The nave became relatively shorter, the projection of the transept less evident, and the chancel larger.

Fig. 8.9
The chancel becomes larger.

Fig. 8.10
The ribbed vault was much lighter and more elegant, which enabled architects to raise vaults much higher, and the wall became a thin shell of stone and glass, with the quality of transparency.

Fig. 8.11
Notre Dame de Paris. The invention of the flying buttress, a heavy arched pier of stone on the outside of the church, reduced the thickness of the heavy wall.

Fig. 8.12
The central nave. Colored glass transformed natural light into a mysterious medium which seemed to prove the immediate presence of God.

 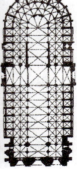

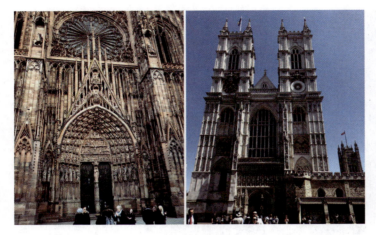

Fig. 8.13 (left) Cathedrale Notre-Dame, France, 1176-1439 The massive wall is reduced to a network of abstract lines and hence is dissolved and becomes transparent.

Fig. 8.14 (right) Westminster Abbey, 1220-1517 rebuilt, London

This enabled architects to raise vaults much higher than was possible in Romanesque architecture. In addition, the pointed arch gave a greater flexibility to architectural form. (Fig. 8.8-Fig. 8.10)

The invention of the flying buttress, a heavy arched pier of stone on the outside of the church, reduced the thickness of the heavy wall and, as a result, cathedral exteriors lost any trace of massive enclosure. Consequently, the wall was designed as a thin shell of stone and glass, with the quality of transparency. This transparency offers a new interpretation to Christian light symbolism. In the cathedrals colored glass transformed natural light into a mysterious medium which seemed to prove the immediate presence of God. (Fig. 8.11-Fig. 8.14)

The purpose of the style was mystical and spiritual. It looked up to heaven to reflect the divine light of God. The style spread rapidly.

Whereas the exterior of the Early Christian church is a continuous, enclosing envelope, and the Romanesque church a stronghold, in the Gothic church, the building is a diaphanous skeleton whose mass is reduced to a network of abstract lines. The wall is dissolved and becomes transparent. Hence, fully developed medieval church no longer appears as a refuge, but functions as the center of a meaningful, spatial organism. A new relationship between the church and its surroundings was established.

8.3 Other Achievements

8.3.1 Education and Learning

Trade grew throughout Europe as the dangers of travel were reduced, and steady economic growth resumed. Cathedral schools and monasteries ceased to be the sole sources of education in the 11th century, when universities were established in major European cities. Literacy became available to a wider class of people, and there were major advances in art, sculpture, music, and architecture. Large cathedrals were built across Europe, first in the Romanesque, and later in the more decorative Gothic style.

The first European medieval institutions generally considered to be universities were established in Italy, France, and England in the late 11th and the 12th centuries for the study of arts, law, medicine, and theology, e.g. Bologna University (1088), University of Paris (1180), Oxford University (1168). These universities evolved from much older Christian cathedral schools or monastic schools, in which monks and nuns taught classes and it is difficult to define the date at which they became true universities.

As defined by medieval specialist, the medieval university is an institution of higher learning which was also a legally autonomous corporation of teachers and students, and by this definition universities are the unique creation of the West European High Middle Ages. By this definition, neither Early Medieval cathedral or monastic schools, nor Byzantine, Islamic, Chinese or Indian institutions of higher learning were universities, since they lacked the corporate legal structure of the later Western European universities.

8.3.2 Science and Technology

The increased contact with the Islamic world in Spain and Sicily, and during the Crusade, allowed Europeans access to scientific Arabic and Greek texts. The development of the medieval university coincided with the widespread reintroduction of Aristotle from Byzantine and Arab scholars. In fact, the European university put Aristotelian and other natural science texts into its curriculum. The European universities aided in the translation and spreading of these texts.

During the 12th and 13th century in Europe, there was a radical change in the rate of new inventions, innovations in the ways of managing traditional means of production, and economic growth. The period saw major technological advances, including the invention of cannon, spectacles, and windmills, and the cross-cultural introduction of gunpowder, silk, compass and etc. from the east. There were also great improvements to ships and clock. The latter advances made possible the dawn of the Age of Exploration. At the same time, huge numbers of Greek and Arabic works on medicine and the sciences were translated and distributed throughout Europe. Aristotle especially became very important, and his rational and logical approach to knowledge influenced the scholars at the newly forming universities which were absorbing and disseminating the new knowledge during the 12th century intellectual revival.

8.4 Late Middle Ages

The Late Middle Ages (1300−1499) is a term used by historians to describe European history in the period of the 14th and 15th centuries

Around 1300, centuries of European prosperity and growth came to a halt. During this time, agriculture was affected by a climate change. A series of famines and plagues, such as the Great Famine of 1315−1317 and the Black Death peaking between 1348 and 1350, a disease that spread among the populace like wildfire, reduced the population by as much as half according to some estimates. Towns were especially hard-hit because of the crowded conditions. Large areas of land were left sparsely inhabited, and in some places fields were left unworked. Along with depopulation came social unrest and endemic warfare. France and England experienced serious peasant uprisings and the Hundred Years' War. To add to the many problems of the period, the unity of the Catholic Church was shattered by the internal division. Collectively these events are sometimes called the Crisis of the Late Middle Ages.

Despite these crises, the 14th century was also a time of great progress within the arts and sciences. A renewed interest in ancient Greek and Roman texts led to what has later been termed the Italian Renaissance. The Latin translation of Greek and Arabic works of natural science, philosophy and mathematics started in the twelfth-century intellectual revival through contact with Arabs during the Crusade, and the availability of important Greek texts accelerated with the capture of Constantinople by the Ottoman Empire, when many Byzantine scholars had to seek refuge in the West, particularly Italy.

In fact, scientific activities were carried out throughout the Middle Ages in areas as diverse as astronomy, medicine, and mathematics. Whereas the ancient cultures of the world had developed many of the foundations of science, it was during the Middle Ages that the scientific method was born and science became a formal discipline separate from philosophy. There were scientific discoveries throughout the world, as in the Islamic world, in the Mediterranean basin, China and India, while from the 12th century onwards, the scientific development in Western Europe began to catch up again.

Combined with this influx of classical ideas was the invention of printing which facilitated dissemination of the printed word and democratized learning. These two things would later lead to the Protestant Reformation.

Toward the end of the period, an era of discovery began (Age of Discovery). The growth of the Ottoman Empire, culminating in the fall of Constantinople in 1453, cut off trading possibilities with the east. Europeans were forced to discover new trading routes, as was the case with Columbus's travel to the Americas in 1492, and Vasco da Gama's circumnavigation of India and Africa in 1498. Their discoveries strengthened the economy and power of European nations.

The changes brought about by these developments have caused many scholars to see it as leading to the end of the Middle Ages, and the beginning of the modern world. However, to other scholars, this division is somewhat artificial since ancient learning was never entirely absent from European society, and there was continuity between the Classical and the Modern age. Some historians prefer not to speak of the Late Middle Ages at all, but rather see the 14th century Renaissance as a direct transition to the Modern Era.

In medieval Europe the Church was one of the most powerful institutions. Art and literature, law, education, and politics were preserved in the teachings of the Church. The Church helped found many of the great universities of Europe and monasteries, some of which continue to exist today, and sponsored art, music and architecture. As the Church grew more powerful and wealthy, large cathedrals were constructed throughout Europe.

The people of the Middle Ages had a rich culture and produced many advances in art, literature, science and medicine, and paved the way for the ideas that would become the beginning of the Renaissance. The thousand years between the 5th and

15th centuries is called the Middle Ages or the Medieval period. This period began and ended for different countries at different times across Europe. It also affected different areas of the continent in different ways.

New Words and Expressions

guild　*n.* 中世纪的行会
Crusade　*n.* 十字军东征
ecclesiastical　*a.* 基督教会的
archbishop　*n.* 大主教
conviction　*n.* 信念；信仰
apprenticeship　*n.* 学徒身份；学徒期
reign　*n.* （某君主的）统治时期
burgher　*n.* 市民
proliferation　*n.* （生物学）增殖；增生（物）
ribbed vault　*n.* 带肋穹顶；扇形穹顶
flying buttress　*n.* 飞扶壁
diaphanous　*a.* 轻薄半透明的
skeleton　*n.* （建筑物、桥梁等的）框架；骨架
dissolve　*vi. & vt.* 变弱；消失
theology　*n.* 神学
autonomous　*a.* 自治的
corporation　*n.* 法人；社团；公司
influx　*n.* 大量涌进
dissemination　*n.* 散布；传播（消息、观点等）
circumnavigation　*n.* 环绕（地球）航行
endemic　*a.* 地方性的
Protestant Reformation　宗教改革
culminate　*vi.* 达到高峰（顶点）

Chapter Nine   Renaissance

导读

  文艺复兴囊括了对古典文化的重新学习与研究，大师们"游学"罗马，在废墟中寻找被遗忘的古典著作，在建筑中探寻几何结构的明晰构图与和谐的比例关系，特别是，对透视法和解剖学的研究使绘画在表现三维空间和人物形象方面更为精准真实，栩栩如生。

  人文主义大师再次发现了现世生活中的美学意义，不再把美好愿望寄托于彼岸的来生，他们开始注重现世生活和人的价值，在艺术创作上像古希腊人那样着力表现人体之美。从此，他们不再是工匠和艺人，而是享有崇高社会地位的艺术家和人文主义大师。

  此时的意大利不像法国、英国和西班牙那样已经成为强大的王国，其土地上林立的城市共和国已进入高度文明的社会，充满了创造力和竞争力，市民享有相当的自由和舒适的生活。财富的积累使人们有钱有闲赞助艺术创作，接受艺术熏陶，财富与艺术的结合带来了文化与艺术的空前繁荣。

  意大利文艺复兴时期的建筑与艺术大致可分为两个阶段：以佛罗伦萨为代表的文艺复兴早期和以罗马为代表的文艺复兴盛期。文艺复兴风格的建筑多采用古典建筑元素构筑，例如，古典柱式、壁柱、山墙、檐部、拱券和穹顶等，平面布局和立面构图讲究对称与和谐的比例关系。

  The Renaissance was a period of great cultural changes and achievements in Europe that spanned roughly from the 14th to the 17th century, marking the transition between Medieval and Early Modern Europe. The term Renaissance is in essence a modern one that came into being in the nineteenth century, in the work of historians. Since the changes of the Renaissance were not uniformed across Europe, the term is generally used to refer to the historic era.

  There is a general, but not unchallenged, consensus that the Renaissance began in Florence, Tuscany in the period of the Late Middle Ages. Various theories have been proposed to account for its origin and characteristics, focusing on a variety of factors including the social and civic peculiarities of Florence at the time; its political structure;

the patronage of its dominant family, the Medici; and the migration of Greek scholars and texts to Italy following the Fall of Constantinople at the hands of the Ottoman Empire.

As a cultural movement, the Renaissance has profoundly affected European intellectual life in the early modern period. Beginning in Italy, and spreading to the rest of Europe by the 16th century, its influence affected literature, philosophy, art, politics, science, religion, and other aspects of intellectual inquiry.

The Renaissance encompassed a resurgence of learning based on classical sources, and gradual but widespread educational reform; however, many aspects of Italian culture and society remained largely medieval. The Renaissance did not come into full swing until the end of the 14th century. The word Renaissance, French for "rebirth", is best known for the renewed interest in the culture of classical antiquity. These changes, while significant, were concentrated in the elite, and for the vast majority of the population life was little changed from the Middle Ages.

Traditionally, this era is viewed as a bridge between the Middle Ages and the Modern era. Although the Renaissance saw revolutions in many intellectual pursuits, as well as social and political upheaval, it is perhaps best known for its artistic developments and the contributions of such polymaths as Leonardo da Vinci and Michelangelo, who inspired the term "Renaissance man".

9.1 Socio-economic Background

The 14th century saw a series of great disasters that caused the European economy to go into recession. Climate change caused the agricultural output to decline significantly, leading to repeated famines. The Hundred Years' War between England and France disrupted trade throughout northwest Europe. The war in the east was also disrupting trade routes, as the Ottoman Empire began to expand throughout the region. The most devastating was the Black Death that decimated the populations of the densely populated cities of Northern Italy and returned at intervals thereafter. Paradoxically, some of these disasters would help establish the Renaissance. First, the reduced population was much better fed, and had more surplus money to spend on luxury goods like art and architecture. Additionally, the collapse of older banking families opened the way for the Medici to rise to prominence in Florence.

9.1.1 Italian Cities

In the thirteenth century, Europe in general was experiencing an economic boom.

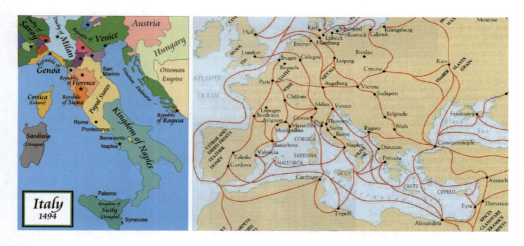

Fig. 9.1
Italy did not exist as a political entity; instead, it was divided into a number of independent kingdoms and republics. The city-states of Northern Italy were prosperous through trade with the rest of Europe.

While Italy did not exist as a political entity, instead, it was divided into a number of independent kingdoms and republics and consequently without the same political power as France, Spain or England. However its cities, owing mainly to their independence, were in a far more advanced state of civilization than the cities of other countries, and their inhabitants enjoyed a degree of comfort and luxury unknown elsewhere. (Fig. 9.1)

The dignified traditions of Roman planning had never been entirely abandoned, the fine scale of open spaces of numerous squares still existed, and the noble paved Roman roads branched in all directions, compared with the unpaved lanes of London and the muddy labyrinths of Paris. Its society was based on merchants and commerce, with democratic features, which was conducive to academic and artistic advancement.

By the end of the Middle Ages, central Italy—the heartland of the Roman Empire, and southern Italy, were poorer than the north. Rome was a city of ancient ruins. The city-states of Northern Italy were prosperous through trade with the rest of Europe. The Crusade had built lasting trade links to Western Asia. The demand for luxury goods led to an increase in trade, which led to greater numbers of tradesmen becoming wealthy. This change also gave the merchants almost complete control of the governments of the Italian city-states, again enhancing trade. Modern commercial infrastructure also developed, with international banking system, systematized foreign exchange market, insurance, and government debt. Florence became the center of this financial industry.

The great powers in Italy of this period were Milan and Venice in the north, Florence and Rome in the center, and Naples in the south.

Florence became one of the wealthiest cities of Northern Italy, due mainly to its woolen textile production, under the supervision of its dominant trade guild. The government of Florence rested in the hands of the seven great Guilds. All the leading merchants and traders were members of these societies. The wealthy burghers were the patrons, and the architects, sculptors, painters and goldsmiths were their employees. The guild that exercised most influence over art in the city was the guild of wool dressers, which sponsored the construction of the dome on the Cathedral. Early in the fifteenth century, the Republic of Florence had become not only one of the most powerful states in Italy, but also the acknowledged chief center for everything concerning literature and fine arts.

Although Florence was a republic, one Florentine family in particular stands out above all others, not only as the most powerful in the history of the city, but also as one of the most famous in the whole Italy. The Medici were originally merchants in Florence, and turned their business from trade to the lucrative money-lending. Acquiring great wealth and influence they rose rapidly, and practically became absolute rulers of the town. Nor was their influence confined to Florence alone. The Medici became the chief bankers to the princes of Europe. For over two hundred years, it remained the ruling dynasty in Florence.

Likewise, the position of Italian cities as great trading centers made them intellectual crossroads. Merchants brought with them ideas from far corners of the globe, particularly Western Asia. Venice was Europe's gateway to trade with the East, and a producer of fine glass, while Florence was a capital of textiles. The wealth such business brought to Italy meant large public and private artistic projects could be commissioned. The wealthy now began to have leisure to meet and talk, to form societies and discuss art, politics and philosophical questions. They became more refined in their behavior, spending time listening to music and dancing. A new attitude developed towards the human being, which was different from the pessimistic medieval view. People began to admire human beings and their abilities, just as the Greeks had done.

A difference between the artistic craftsmen of Italy in the fourteenth and fifteenth centuries and his contemporary in other European countries is that the latter followed but one craft; he was a carpenter, or a painter. The Florentine was accomplished in many crafts. He undertook, as chance offered, the work and duties of architect, painter, sculptor and goldsmith. His versatility was largely owing to a kind of workshop training, in which men obtained their training in a wide variety of work. An apprentice in those days learnt many trades. The master and his apprentices carried out, whatever clients were willing to entrust to him. Leonardo da Vinci, a late Renaissance artist, is most commonly known for the *Mona Lisa*, but he was also an engineer and a scientist.

The artists of the Early Renaissance used scientific tools (like linear perspective and the study of anatomy, as well as geometry) to make their art more naturalistic. (Fig. 9.2) They began to demand that the society think of them as more than just skilled manual laborers.

Through careful observation of nature and anatomical dissections, Renaissance artists had found the means to produce realistic representations of what they saw on the flat surface of a wall (in the case of frescoes) or on a wooden panel or paper (in the case of drawings and paintings).

During the Renaissance, architects trained as humanists helped raise the status of their profession from skilled laborer to artist. In the early Renaissance, artists were seen as craftsmen with little prestige or recognition. By the later Renaissance, the top figures had great influence and could charge great fees. They became aristocrats.

9.1.2 Patronage

Renaissance art flourished largely because of the patronage, or financial support, of wealthy citizens and the church. By purchasing numerous works of art, Renaissance men provided a livelihood for many painters, sculptors, and architects. A flourishing trade in Renaissance art developed. It was also the Renaissance humanist desire to imitate and revive the beauty of ancient Greece, and to have that beauty surround them in their daily lives, that produced the wealth of superb art.

During Renaissance, money and art went hand in hand. Artists depended totally on patrons while the patrons needed money to sustain geniuses. Wealth was brought to Italy in the 14th, 15th and 16th centuries by expanding trade into Asia and Europe. Silver mining increased the flow of money. Wealthy families—the Medici of Florence, the Gonzaga of Mantua, the Farnese in Rome, the Sforzas in Milan—gathered around them people of learning and talent, promoting the skills and creating employment for the most talented artists and architects of their day.

9.2 Humanism

The Italian trade routes that covered the Mediterranean and beyond were also major conduits of culture and knowledge. In medieval times, works that embodied the classical learning of the Greeks had flowed into Western Europe. The Crusade led to some European contact with classical learning. But more importantly, through Moorish Spain Arabic-language works were introduced into Europe. From Egypt and the Western Asia, the scientific, philosophical, and mathematical thinking of the Arabs entered Northern Italy. The conquest of Constantinople by the Turks in 1453 had more important results. It drove from that city numerous Greek scholars, who, with such manuscripts and works of art, some of which had been lost for centuries in the West, found a welcome and a refuge in Italy, and especially in Florence. Their scholarship led the Florentines to a true understanding of ancient Greek literature.

In contrast to the High Middle Ages, when Latin scholars focused almost entirely on studying Greek and Arabic works of natural science, philosophy and mathematics, Renaissance scholars were most interested in recovering, interpreting, and assimilating the language, literature, learning and values of ancient Greece and Rome. All-round development of individuals became the ideal of humanists. Renaissance thinkers sought out in Europe's monastic libraries and the crumbling Byzantine Empire the works of antiquity, typically written in Latin or ancient Greek. One of the greatest achievements of Renaissance scholars was to bring this entire class of Greek cultural works back into Western Europe for the first time since late antiquity. Renaissance artists were encouraged, in the atmosphere of humanist optimism, to excel the achievements of the ancient time.

During the Renaissance there was an increase in rationalism and lessening of faith. The medieval idea that this life is just a preparation for a better life after death was questioned. One theory proposed that the devastation caused by the Black Death resulted in a shift in the world view of people in 14th-century Italy, causing people to dwell more on their lives on Earth, rather than on spirituality and the afterlife. Humanists began to realize the importance of human beings themselves and the value of this life, justifying their pursuit of happiness and enjoyment, although religion still played a dominant role in social and private life, many art works were devoted to God or patronaged by the church.

In the works of art, human body was the most beautiful thing to paint. The Sculpture of David indicates the study of human anatomy was enormously important for Renaissance artists. The Renaissance aesthetic is apparent in the careful and accurate depiction of the human body. Once again, as in classical antiquity (ancient Greece and Rome) the human figure was considered beautiful. (Fig.9.4)

The Vitruvian Man, "The proportions of the human body according to Vitruvius" is a drawing by Leonardo da Vinci around 1490. The drawing, which is in pen and ink on paper, depicts a man in two superimposed positions with his arms and legs apart and inscribed in a circle and square. The drawing is based on the correlations of ideal human proportions with geometry described by the ancient Roman architect Vitruvius, who described the human figure as being the principal source of proportion among the Classical orders of architecture. Vitruvius determined that the ideal body should be eight heads high. Leonardo's drawing is traditionally named in honor of the architect. (Fig. 9.3)

9.3 Development of the Renaissance

It remains much debated why the Renaissance began in Italy. Most historians agree that the ideas that characterized the Renaissance had their origin in late 13th century Florence. Others see the general competition between artists and polymaths such as Brunelleschi, Ghiberti, Donatello, and Masaccio for artistic commissions as sparking the creativity of the Renaissance in the 1400s.

The unique political structures and social climate allowed the emergence of this cultural creativity. Italy was divided into a number of city states and territories, each with their own form of government, which was dominated by commercial elite. It was this group that was the main patron of, and audience for, Renaissance culture. Below them, there was a large class of artisans and guild members who lived comfortable lives and had significant power in the republican governments. This was in sharp contrast to the rest of Europe where artisans were firmly in the lower class. Literate and educated, this group participated in the Renaissance culture.

Although northern Italy was the most urbanized region of Europe, three quarters of the people were still rural peasants. For this section of the population, life was essentially unchanged from the Middle Ages.

9.3.1 Why Did Renaissance Start in Florence?

It has long been a matter of debate why the Renaissance began in Florence, and not elsewhere in Italy. Scholars have noted several features unique to Florentine cultural life which may have caused such a cultural movement. Many have emphasized

106 An Introduction to Western Culture and Art

Fig. 9.2
Pietro Perugino's usage of perspective in fresco at the Sistine Chapel (1481–1482)

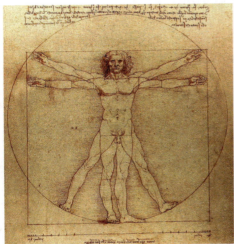 

Fig. 9.3 (left)
The Vitruvian Man
Leonardo da Vinci tried to draw the perfectly proportioned man.

Fig. 9.4 (right)
The Sculpture of David, Michelangelo 1505

Fig. 9.5
The Uffizi Gallery

the role played by the Medici, a banking family—the largest bank in Europe during the 15th century, in patronizing and stimulating the arts.

The biggest accomplishments of the Medici were in the sponsorship of art and architecture. The Medici were responsible for the majority of Florentine art during their reign. In architecture, the Medici were responsible for some notable features of Florence, including the Uffizi Gallery, the Boboli Gardens, the Belvedere, and the Palazzo Medici. (Fig. 9.5–Fig. 9.7) The Medici family was the patron for an enormous amount of art works, encouraging his countryman to commission works from Florence's leading artists, including Leonardo da Vinci, Sandro Botticelli, and Michelangelo Buonarroti.

In addition to commissions for art and architecture, the Medici were prolific collectors and today their acquisitions form the core of the Uffizi museum in Florence. Although none of the Medici themselves were scientists, the family is well known to have been the patrons of the famous Galileo Galilei, an Italian astronomer, mathematician and physicist, who tutored multiple generations of Medici children.

The Renaissance was certainly underway before the Medici family came to power. Some historians suggest that Florence was the birthplace of the Renaissance as a result of luck, i.e. because "Great Men" were born there by chance. Da Vinci, Botticelli and Michelangelo were all born in Tuscany. Other historians have contended that these "Great Men" were only able to rise to prominence because of the prevailing cultural conditions at the time.

9.3.2 The Renaissance in Rome

When many other states in Italy were undertaking vast building projects and Florence was a scene of commercial and architectural activity, Rome was a decayed city much reduced in size and population by famine and poverty. Monuments were devastated by fire, earthquake and neglect, and practically all the churches were in a ruinous state, with the exile of the Popes. On the return of the Pope in 1377, the redevelopment of the area and a great revival of life in the city started. The Vatican became the residence of the Pope, adjoining the Early Christian basilica on the site of the burial place of S. Peter. On Alberti's advice a city plan was formulated and put into practice.

However, these intellectual and cultural activities, at the peak of their achievement, had been disrupted by the sack of Rome by Spanish imperial troops in 1527, and these pursuits came to a standstill.

Fig. 9.6
The Palazzo Medici

Fig. 9.7
Mirror hall, The Palazzo Medici

Fig. 9.8
Pazzi Chapel. Classical orders and elements such as columns, pilasters, pediments, entablatures, arches, and domes form the vocabulary of Renaissance buildings.

Fig. 9.9 (left)
San Lorenzo

Fig. 9.10 (right)
Interior, San Lorenzo
The Renaissance style places emphasis on symmetry, proportion, geometry and the regularity of parts.

9.4 Renaissance Architecture and Art

Renaissance architecture is the architecture of the period between the early 15th and early 17th centuries in different regions of Europe, in which there was a conscious revival and development of certain elements of ancient Greek and Roman thought and culture. With the rediscovered knowledge from the 1st-century writer Vitruvius, the architectural principles of Antiquity could be observed once more.

The distinguishing features of Classical Roman architecture were adopted by Renaissance architects. However, the forms and purposes of buildings had changed over time, so had the structure of cities. There was no call for enormous sporting facilities and public bath complexes such as the Romans had built. The ancient orders were analyzed and reconstructed to serve new purposes.

Renaissance arts in Italy can be divided into two periods: the early Renaissance period in Florence, and the High Renaissance period in Rome under the "Renaissance Popes". Florence was the first center of the Renaissance. The most important men of letters of the early Renaissance were all Florentines. By the fifteenth century, under the patronage of Medici family, the arts of Florence reached its golden age.

The Renaissance spread to Rome only after the middle of the fifteenth century, and was brought to its peak by three "Renaissance Popes". In 1377 the Pope had returned to Rome from exile, and gradually the old city emerged from the misery and low estate to its rightful place amongst the cities and powers of Italy. After the sack of Rome in 1527, the Roman Renaissance gradually declined, and the center shifted to Venice, where Italian Renaissance lingered until the end of the sixteenth century.

9.4.1 The Early Renaissance Period in Florence

Florence was a shining example of the best of the Italian Renaissance. It is in Florence that the new architectural style had its beginning, not slowly evolving in the way that Gothic grew out of Romanesque, but consciously brought to being by particular architects who sought to revive the order of a past "Golden Age". The study of classical antiquity led in particular to the adoption of Classical detail and ornamentation. The scholarly approach to the architecture of the ancient coincided with the general revival of learning.

Italian Renaissance architects based their theories and practices on Classical Roman examples. The Renaissance revival of Classical Rome was as important in architecture as it was in literature. A pilgrimage to Rome to study the ancient

Fig. 9.11
S. Maria Novella. Alberti linked the lower roofs of the aisles to nave using two large scrolls.

Fig. 9.12
Brunelleschi, elevation of Santo Spirito, 1434–1483, and a photo of the actual church
It seems reasonable to assume that Brunelleschi devised the method of perspective to provide a correspondingly accurate representation of physical space to show his clients how it would look after it was built.

buildings and ruins, especially the Colosseum and Pantheon, was considered essential to an architect's training. Classical orders and architectural elements such as columns, pilasters, pediments, entablatures, arches, and domes form the vocabulary of Renaissance buildings. For example, the combination of a dome, pediment and pillars was repeatedly copied. Vitruvius's writings on architecture also influenced the Renaissance definition of beauty in architecture. The Renaissance style places emphasis on symmetry, proportion, geometry and the regularity of parts as they are demonstrated in the architecture of classical antiquity and in particular ancient Roman architecture, of which many examples remained. (Fig. 9.8)

The new architectural philosophy is best demonstrated in the churches of San Lorenzo and San Spirito in Florence, designed by Brunelleschi in about 1425 and 1428 respectively. (Fig. 9.9, Fig. 9.10, Fig. 9.12)Both have the shape of the Latin cross, based on a modular plan. In S. Maria Novella, for the first time, Alberti linked the lower roofs of the aisles to nave using two large scrolls. They were to become a standard Renaissance device for solving the problem of different roof heights and bridge the space between horizontal and vertical surfaces. (Fig. 9.11)

The person generally credited with bringing about the Renaissance view of architecture is Filippo Brunelleschi (1377–1446), who observed that the way one sees regular structures follows a mathematical order—linear perspective. This new technique of mathematical perspective enabled architects to provide a correspondingly accurate representation of physical space on two-dimensional surfaces like a wooden panel or paper, and to show his clients how it would look after it was built.

The development of linear perspective in painting made the representation of three dimensions more authentic. What renaissance artists had achieved through the careful observation of nature and studies of anatomical dissections, which enabled artists to understand the hidden structure of the human body, was the means to recreate the 3-dimensional physical reality of the human form in paintings and frescoes. Renaissance artists also developed other artistic techniques, studying light and shadow to depict the beauty of nature.

Also, the buildings remaining among the ruins of ancient Rome seemed to suggest a fixed proportion applied to all Ancient Roman architecture, which was absent from Gothic buildings. A semi-circular arch in ancient Roman buildings is exactly twice as wide as it is high, while a Gothic pointed arch could be extended upwards or flattened to any proportion that suited the location. Arches of differing angles frequently occurred within the same structure of Gothic style, with no set rules of proportion applied.

In wealthy Florence, the impetus for church-building was more civic than

112 An Introduction to Western Culture and Art

Fig. 9.13
Florence's cathedral and the dome

Fig. 9.14
The dome

Fig. 9.15
The dome of the Pantheon

spiritual. Some major ecclesiastical building works were commissioned, not by the church, but by guilds representing the wealth and power of the city. Brunelleschi's first major architectural commission (in 1418) was for the enormous brick dome to cover the central space of Florence's cathedral, which was designed in the 14th century but left unroofed. As the technology and finance were found to complete it, the rising dome designed by Brunelleschi brought great honor not only to the church but also to the city and its architect. It was for the Florence cathedral that Michelangelo created his famous sculpture of David. The construction of the dome marks the beginning of Renaissance architecture. Brunelleschi borrowed ideas from the ancient ruins and incorporated them into the design of his dome. His daring design utilizes the pointed Gothic arch and Gothic ribs in keeping with the building it surmounts. The dome is in fact a structural solution from Ancient Rome, the dome of the Pantheon. The dome inspired further religious works in Florence. (Fig. 9.13–Fig. 9.15)

9.4.2 The High Renaissance Period in Rome

Developed first in Florence, the Renaissance style quickly spread to other Italian cities and then to France, Germany, England, Russia and elsewhere. Italian Renaissance painting also exercised a dominant influence on subsequent European painting for centuries afterwards.

The Renaissance had a significant effect on Rome, and the new emphasis on Rome as the center of Christian spirituality brought about a boom in the building of churches in Rome. This commenced in the mid 15th century and gained momentum in the 16th century, reaching its peak in the Baroque period. The construction of Sistine Chapel and rebuilding of St Peter's, one of Christendom's most significant churches, was part of this process. The fame of the Sistine Chapel lies mainly in the frescos that decorate the interior, and most particularly the Chapel ceiling and *The Last Judgment* by Michelangelo. St. Peter's was "the greatest creation of the Renaissance", and a great number of architects contributed their skills to it. But at its completion, there was more of Michelangelo's design than of any other architect, before or after him. (Fig. 9.16–Fig. 9.19)

The Tempietto (1502) in the cloister of San Pietro, Rome, designed by Bramante, has been described as "a perfect architectural gem". This small circular temple marks the place where St. Peter was put to death and is the most sacred site in Rome. The building apparently adopts the style of ancient Roman circular temple. (Fig. 9.20)

9.4.3 Cities and Dwellings

The ideal city of the Renaissance no longer expresses a communal form of life,

Fig. 9.16
Sistine Chapel. A team of Renaissance painters created a series of frescos depicting the Life of Moses and the Life of Christ. Michelangelo painted the chapel's ceiling, a project which is regarded as one of the major artistic accomplishments of human civilization.

Fig. 9.17
St. Peter's Basilica. The central space is dominated both externally and internally by one of the largest domes in the world. The dome is inspired by that of the huge circular Roman temple, the Pantheon. The main difference between the dome of St. Peter's and that of the Pantheon is that the dome of the Pantheon is supported by a continuous wall, while that of the St Peter's is set on a drum supported only by four large piers.

Fig. 9.18
Dome of St. Peter's Basilica

Chapter Nine   Renaissance   115

Fig. 9.19
The nave of St. Peter's Basilica. The basilica is in a Latin cross form, with an elongated nave, but a centrally planned structure is still in evidence. The entire interior is lavishly decorated with marble, reliefs, architectural sculpture and gilding.

Fig. 9.20
The Tempietto

Fig. 9.21
At the centre of the ideal city is the palace of noble families connected to a large piazza.

Fig. 9.22
The staircase to the reading room

Fig. 9.23
The reading room
Classical elements such as columns, pilasters, pediments, entablatures are repeatedly copied. The Laurentian Library is renowned for its architecture, designed by Michelangelo.

9.24
Palazzo Farnese. The building is surmounted by a cornice. There is a regular repetition of openings on each floor, and the centrally placed door is marked by a rusticated surround.

such as the late medieval town, but forms the centre of a small autocratic state. At the centre of the ideal city is the palace of noble families connected to a large piazza. Renaissance architecture is a product of an urban civilization.

Through Humanism, civic pride and the promotion of civil peace and order were seen as the marks of citizenship. This led to the building of structures such as Brunelleschi's Hospital of the Innocents with its elegant colonnade forming a link between the charitable building and the public square, and the Laurentian Library where the collection of books established by the Medici family could be consulted by scholars.

Domestic buildings are often surmounted by a cornice. There is a regular repetition of openings on each floor, and the centrally placed door is marked by a feature such as a balcony, or rusticated surround. (Fig. 9.24) The Palazzo Medici Riccardi, designed by Michelozzo, is classical in the details of its pedimented window and recessed doors, and the orders of three rusticated levels are created. (Fig. 9.6) Alberti's Palazzo Rucellai applied the classical orders of columns to the façade on the three levels. Palladio's best known domestic buildings is la Rotonda, a centrally planned house with a domed central hall and four identical facades, each with a temple-like portico like that of the Pantheon in Rome. Palladio was to transform the architectural style of both palaces and churches by taking Classical elements

While Gothic church created a spiritual and mystical world, striving to reach the heaven, the Renaissance architects were more interested in proportion, clear lines and mathematical relationships. Domes replaced spires, horizontal lines replaced the vertical one. Architects were looking for styles that pleased the eye and satisfied a sense of proportion. They hoped to create structures that would appeal to both emotion and reason. Once again, the emphasis is on aesthetic and not spiritual appeal.

The pre-eminence of Italy continued until the end of the sixteenth century. Then its commerce declined, and other countries achieved supremacy.

New Words and Expressions

consensus *n.* 一致；合意
peculiarity *n.* 独有的特点；独特性
patronage *n.* 赞助
encompass *vt.* 包含；包括；覆盖
resurgence *n.* 复活
antiquity *n.* 古代；年代久远
elite *n.* 精英
upheaval *n.* 动乱；巨变
polymath *n.* 博学大师
recession *n.* （经济）衰退期
devastate *vt.* 破坏；毁灭
decimate *vt.* 大批杀死
paradoxically *adv.* 自相矛盾的
surplus *n.* 剩余；过剩
entity *n.* 实体
labyrinth *n.* 迷宫；曲径
conducive to 有益于
dresser *n.* 服装师
lucrative *adj.* 可赚大钱的；利润丰厚的
accomplished *adj.* 有造诣的；有才艺的
versatility *n.* 多才多艺
apprentice *n.* 学徒
entrust *vt.* 委托
linear perspective *n.* 直线透视（图）
anatomy *n.* 解剖学
aristocrat *n.* 贵族
sustain *vt.* 支持；支撑
conduit *n.* 管道；导管
assimilate *vt.* 吸收；同化

crumble　*vi.* 衰落；崩溃；瓦解；破灭
devastation　*n.* 破坏；毁灭
depiction　*n.* 描绘；刻画
Vitruvius　维特鲁威（古罗马工程师和建筑师）
superimposed　*a.* 使重叠的；使叠加的
inscribe　*vt.* 刻写；印
correlation　*n.* 相互关系
artisan　*n.* 工匠（craftsman）
prolific　*a.* 多产的；多成果的
exile　*n.* 流放
adjoin　*vt.* 贴近；比邻
sack　*n.* 劫掠；洗劫
pilaster　*n.* 壁柱；半露柱（a rectangular column that is attached to a wall and that is used for decoration or support）
pediment　*n.* 山墙柱廊上的三角形檐饰；门窗上弧形/三角形檐饰
entablature　*n.* 古典柱式的檐部（a horizontal part in classical architecture that rests on the columns and consists of architrave, frieze, and cornice）
modular　*a.* 模块化的；有标准组件的
scrolls　*n.* 涡卷形（a decoration that looks like the curled ends of a scroll）
authentic　*a.* 真实的
impetus　*n.* 推动；动力
surmount　*vt.* 置于某物顶端
momentum　*n.* 势头；动力
Christendom　*n.* 基督教徒（all Christian people）
cloister　*n.* 回廊（a covered passage with arches around a square garden, usually forming part of a cathedral, convent, or monastery）
autocratic　*a.* 独裁统治的
piazza　*n.* 广场（a public square, especially in an Italian town）
cornice　*n.* 飞檐（the decorative top edge of a building or column）
rusticated　*a.* 粗琢的
recessed　*a.* 凹进的
façade　*n.* 正面；立面
la Rotonda　*n.* 圆厅别墅
portico　*n.* 门廊；柱廊（a row of columns supporting a roof at the entrance of a building）
eminence　*n.* 卓越；出众

Chapter Ten　The Seventeenth Century

导读

17世纪，随着大西洋海上贸易的发展，欧洲的发展重心由地中海沿岸转向西北欧，欧洲强国在海外的贸易和殖民扩张中获得了巨额的财富。

与此同时，为了对抗16世纪在欧洲兴起的宗教改革运动，艺术成为罗马天主教发起的反宗教改革运动的中心内容，宏大的建筑计划在天主教国家全面实施，其宗旨是展示罗马天主教的实力和财富，通过艺术表现宗教的主题与感染力。这一时期兴建的教堂、城市广场和花园别墅追求宏大壮丽的风貌，史称巴洛克风格。艺术在宗教、国家事务和美化生活方面都发挥了重要作用。

巴洛克风格的主要特征为：追求新奇与华丽的视觉效果，赋予建筑以动态感，波折扭转，不规则造型，将色彩、光影、雕塑和绘画等装饰艺术融为一体。

10.1 Socio-economic Background

The 16th century saw the flowering of the Renaissance in the rest of the West and a fundamental transformation in scientific ideas across mathematics, physics, astronomy, biology, medicine, chemistry and in scientific investigation. The widely held picture of the universe also changed. Polish astronomer Copernicus suggested the Sun as the center of the universe. The Italian astronomer Galileo developed telescope technology. In England, Newton pioneered the science of physics. These events led to the so-called scientific revolution, which began in Europe towards the end of the Renaissance era and continued through the late 18th century, influencing the intellectual social movement known as the Enlightenment. The scientific revolution led to the establishment of modern science.

The 17th century is probably the most important century in the making of the modern world. During this period strong centralized European states entered into worldwide international competition for wealth and power, accelerating the pace of colonization in America and Asia. The Dutch, French, Spanish, Portuguese, English, and others, all struggled to maintain and extend colonies and trading-posts in distant corners of the globe, with profound and permanent consequences for the whole world. The military tactics and technology improved to the point where European arms were superior to any in the world.

During the 15th and 16th centuries European trade had revolved largely around the Mediterranean, and the Renaissance was dominated by Italian artists and intellectuals. With the Ottoman Empire taking hold of Constantinople in 1453, the trading routes to the east were cut off. Europeans were forced to discover new trading routes.

In the 17th century, the Atlantic trade routes became far more important, the center of economic gravity shifted to Northern Europe, and it was there that intellectual, agricultural and industrial developments moved most rapidly. The application of scientific knowledge and mathematics to navigation and ship-building were intimately connected with the expansion of trade.

The Reformation

The other major movement in the West in the sixteenth century was the Reformation, which would profoundly change the West and end its religious unity. Renaissance coincided with the Religious Reformation. In the Middle Ages, the Roman Catholic Church became increasingly powerful and had virtually become the only religion of Western Europe by the 15th century. The popes of the Catholic Church had much of the same power as temporal rulers did. Naturally, this power led to abuses and church corruption. During the Renaissance, the authority of the Church was challenged, and its evils attacked, as a result of the rise of European nationalism and the new learning. The nations were often angry at the interference of the Popes in their affairs and many people grew discontented with the way the church was run and wanted reforms. In Germany, Martin Luther was one of many who called for moral reform within the Church. The Religious Reformation resulted in a split of the church into the Catholic and the Protestant churches.

By 1650, the religious map of Europe had been redrawn. Scandinavia, Iceland, north Germany, part of Switzerland, the Netherlands and Britain were Protestant, while the rest of the West remained Catholic. (Fig. 10.1)

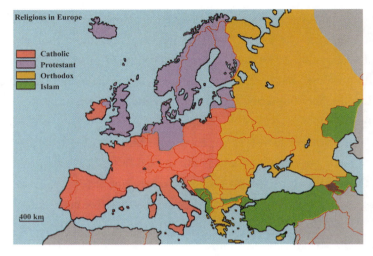

Fig. 10.1
Religious map of Europe

The Reformation brought about a counter-attack from the Catholic Church, called the Counter-Reformation, which was carried in four ways: by war, by spiritual regeneration of the Catholic Church, by education, and through art.

10.2 Baroque Architecture and Art

The Baroque style, prevalent from the early 17th century to the early 18th century, began in Italy and developed in response to the Reformation, a movement that started in 16th century within the Catholic Church to reform itself. If Florence is the ideal city of the Renaissance, then Rome is the ideal city of the Baroque.

Baroque art is often seen as part of the Counter-Reformation—the artistic element of the revival of spiritual life in the Roman Catholic Church. Religion determined many aspects of Baroque art. The church had decided that art should communicate religious themes in direct and emotional involvement. Art was to serve as a means of combating the spread of Protestantism and stimulating the public's faith in the church. To this end the church employed emotional, realistic, and dramatic art to propagate the faith. The Baroque style that evolved from this program was both sensuous and spiritual. Baroque church ceilings thus dissolved in painted scenes that presented vivid and illusory views of the religious image, more accessible to the observers, directing the senses toward heavenly concerns. While the dramatic effects of church façade were created to appeal to churchgoers. (Fig. 10.2) The Baroque manifested itself in the context of a new religious expression, and as a visible statement of the wealth and power of the Catholic Church. The Roman Catholic Church was a highly influential patron.

Political situations also influenced art. The development of Baroque art and architecture also coincided with the rise of European colonialism, which brought in huge amounts of wealth. Colonialism required the development of centralized and powerful governments with Spain and France as the first to move in this direction. The absolute monarchies of France and Spain prompted the creation of works that reflected in their size and splendor the majesty of their kings, Louis XIV and Philip IV. Many Baroque artists served kings who tried to realize this goal. Baroque palaces were built on an expanded and monumental scale in order to display the power and grandeur of the centralized state, as was best displayed in the royal palace and gardens at Versailles. At the same time, a prominent and powerful middle class now came to play a role in art patronage. The development of a picture market for the middle class and its taste for realism may be seen in the works of 17th-century French and Dutch paintings.

The popularity and success of the Baroque style was encouraged by the Roman Catholic Church, which wanted art to teach the illiterate by visual means, and to restore its authority. The aristocracy also saw the dramatic style of Baroque architecture and art as a means of impressing visitors and expressing power and control. Religious and political themes were widely explored within the Baroque artistic context.

Pomp and grandeur were important elements of the Baroque art. Baroque art was particularly ornate and elaborate in nature, often using rich, warm colors with dark undertones. Strong contrasts of light and shadow enhance the dramatic effects of many paintings, sculptures and church facade. The ceiling fresco was a particularly important medium for baroque painters. Baroque buildings, with their undulating walls and decorative surface elements, imply motion. Intense spirituality is often present in works of baroque art

Baroque art in many ways was similar to Renaissance art and can be seen as a more elaborate and dramatic re-adaptation of late Renaissance art. Developed as somewhat of a continuation of the Renaissance, Baroque architecture took the humanist Roman vocabulary of Renaissance architecture and used it in a new fashion, expressing the triumph of the church and state.

Taken literally, the term means "irregular". Baroque Architecture is characterized by free and sculptural use of the classical orders and ornament, and the dramatic

Fig. 10.2
The Church of the Gesu in Rome
Its façade is the first truly Baroque façade, introducing the Baroque style into architecture. Long, narrow naves are replaced by broader, occasionally circular forms.

Fig. 10.3
San Andrea della Valle, Rome (1590–1650), one of the three great 17th century preaching churches (the others being the Gesù and the Chiesa Nuova) built by Counter-Reformation religious orders.

The external façade is often characterized by a dramatic central projection and the interior is often no more than a shell for painting and sculpture.

combined effects of architecture, sculpture, painting, and the decorative arts. The new architectural concerns for color, light and shade, sculptural values and intensity are manifested in Baroque. Baroque art and architecture strove to create an atmosphere of infinity, light, emotion and theatricality. (Fig. 10.3-Fig. 10.6)

Important features of Baroque architecture include:
（1）*Long, narrow naves are replaced by broader, occasionally circular forms.*
（2）*Dramatic use of light, either strong light-and-shade contrasts, or uniform lighting by means of several windows.*
（3）*Large-scale ceiling frescoes.*
（4）*The external façade is often characterized by a dramatic central projection.*
（5）*The interior is often no more than a shell for painting and sculpture.*
（6）*There are no corners in the usual sense of the term, as the wall system is carried on in a curve where corners would have been.*

The Baroque world may be characterized as a great theatre, and the most splendid of the Baroque "theatre" is undoubtedly St. Peter's Square, built in 1675-1677 by the great master of Baroque art, Gian Lorenzo Bernini. It is a supreme example of space composition and functioned as the principal focus of the Catholic world. The symbolic meaning is best expressed in Bernini's words: Since the church of St. Peter is the mother of nearly all the others, it has to have colonnades, as if stretching out its arms maternally to receive Catholics, to reunite them to the Church, to enlighten them in the true faith. (Fig. 10.7, Fig. 10.8)

Instead of being a static, finished form, St. Peter's square is simultaneously closed and open. While clearly defined, its oval shape creates an expansion along the transverse axis, interacting with the world beyond, and this intention is emphasized by the "transparent" colonnades. The obelisk in the square serves as the node where all the directions meet and are connected with the longitudinal axis which leads to the church. The square becomes the real "meeting place of all mankind", and at the same time its message radiates to the entire world.

Outside Italy, Baroque architecture was more widespread and fully developed than the Renaissance style. By the middle of the 17th century, the Baroque style had found its secular expression in the form of grand palaces, first in France and then throughout Europe.

Fig. 10.4
Royal Chapel, Palace of Versailles.
There are no corners in the usual sense of the term, as the wall system is carried on in a curve.

Fig. 10.5 (left)
Santa Maria Maddalena, Rome Curves and decoration were added to the straight classical lines and form, manifesting a movement.

Fig. 10.6 (right)
The Trevi Fountain is the largest Baroque fountain in Rome,1732–1762. Free and sculptural use of the classical orders and ornament, and the dramatic combined effects of architecture and sculpture.

Fig. 10.7
St. Peter's Square
It had to have colonnades, as if stretching out its arms maternally to receive Catholics.

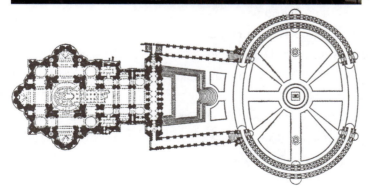

Fig. 10.8
Floor Plan
St. Peter's Square is simultaneously closed and open.

The two most popular types of architectural commission during the Baroque era involved either churches or palaces, and above all royal palaces being especially typical of the period. In addition to such buildings, Baroque architecture was also characterized by what is now known as town planning: the arrangement of cities according to predetermined schemes, and the creation of great parks and gardens around residences of importance.

10.3　French Baroque

During the sixteenth century, France had been torn apart by religious war between Protestants and Catholics, and ravaged by Spanish invasion. In the seventeenth century, Spain declined but France grew increasingly prosperous and powerful until by the end of the century, it was the strongest country in Europe. Its splendid royal court provided the model for all European royalty, and its culture set the standards for educated gentlemen. French Baroque art reached great heights.

During the seventeenth century there was for the first time in history a truly large-scale transformation of the natural landscape. So far nature had been kept outside the cities. A map of Paris from 1740 would show that the whole landscape of the city and its neighboring area have been transformed into a network of centralized systems, with an infinite extension. Most of the development stem from the seventeenth century. However, Rome's urban system was not further developed, and attention instead concentrated on particular monumental projects, such as St. Peter's Square. The development of Paris during the seventeenth century took a very different course from that of Rome.

Symbolic square, directional street and uniform district were characteristic of the city. To strengthen the monarchy and transform the capital city into a worthy expression of the new system, a new element was created, often referred to as royal square, an urban space centered on a statue of the sovereign and surrounded by dwellings, symbolizing a new relationship between the sovereign and his people.

Town planning of this period featured radiating avenues intersecting in squares, which took cues from Baroque garden plans. A ring of broad avenues and centrifugal axes created a new open urban environment. The ideas stem from garden planning, which features the longitudinal axis leading to infinite space. Transverse axes and radiating patterns are introduced to indicate the general open extension of the system.

Fig. 10.9
Schönbrunn Palace, a former imperial summer residence in Vienna, Austria.
Baroque architecture strove to create an atmosphere of theatricality. The city-palace and villa have the horseshoe-shape as their basic structure.

Fig. 10.10
Floor plan of Palace of Versailles and Garden
The palace occupies the very center of the plot and its long wings divide the area into two parts: gardens on one side and town on the other. Transverse axes and radiating patterns are introduced and a ring of broad avenues and centrifugal axes created a new open urban environment.

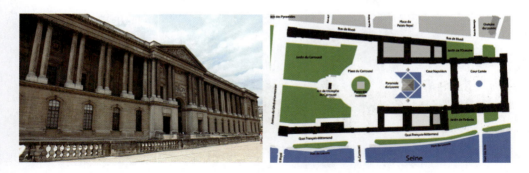

Fig. 10.11 (left)
East wing (1667–1670) of the Louvre Palace
Rhythmically paired columns form a shadowed colonnade with a central pedimented triumphal arch entrance raised on a high defensive base, in a restrained baroque manner.

Fig. 10.12 (right)
Floor plan, the Louvre Palace

Versailles represents the basic properties of the seventeenth-century city: centralization, integration and extension. The palace occupies the very center of the plot and its long wings divide the area into two parts: gardens on one side and town on the other. Both parts are characterized by infinite perspectives centered on the palace: the town is structured by three main avenues radiating away from the center; the layout of the gardens is based on a system of radiating paths and round-points. The surrounding landscape falls into a seemingly limitless system. (Fig. 10.10)

The center of Baroque secular architecture was France, where numerous huge palaces and monasteries were constructed. The city-palace and villa have the horseshoe-shape as their basic structure. (Fig. 10.9) The Louvre Palace, a former royal palace, is a vast complex of wings, which is the result of many phases of building, modification, destruction and restoration. The east wing of the palace (built 1667–1670) is one of the most influential classical facades that have provided models for grand edifices in Europe and America for centuries. (Fig. 10.11, Fig. 10.12) The Palace of Versailles, initially a tiny hunting lodge, was transformed into a marvelous palace for feasts and parties.

From the creation of Versailles, the gardens were an essential part of the new royal residence. They surround the Palace on three sides, north, west and south, and are organized along two principal axes, east-west and north-south. But it was only

Fig. 10.13
The Palace of Versailles

Fig. 10.14
"Grand Perspective", the longitudinal axis leading to infinite space.

Fig. 10.15
Straight avenues of trees, long views, sculptures and fountains dominated the design.

Fig. 10.16
Mirror Hall, Palace of Versailles
The Hall of Mirrors was decorated with marble and gilt bronzes. The principal compositions of the vault depict key episodes in the Dutch War, which marked the high point of the reign of Louis XIV.

Chapter Ten   The Seventeenth Century   131

**Fig. 10.17
Interior decoration**
The interior is often no more than a shell for painting and sculpture.

gradually that the east-west axis was given special importance, becoming in the 1660s the "Grand Perspective" which is still the major axis, made up of parterres decorated with fountains close to the Palace, and prolonged by walks leading to groves with surprising water and greenery effects, they end in vast ornamental lakes reflecting the sky. Straight avenues of trees, long views, sculptures and fountains dominated the design. Architect Louis Le Vau, painter and designer Charles Le Brun and the landscape architect André Le Nôtre created marvels. (Fig. 10.13-Fig. 10.17)

In this period, royal control over artisanal production was established in France; henceforth France would no longer purchase luxury goods from abroad, but would set the standard for quality. This control was also seen in the creation of an academy of painting and sculpture.

New Words and Expressions

tactics   *n.* 策略
temporal   *adj.* 尘世的；世俗的
abuse   *n.* 滥用
Protestant   *n.* 新教；新教徒
Counter-Reformation   *n.* 反宗教改革
Baroque   *n. & a.* 巴洛克风格
combat   *vt.* 战斗、搏斗
propagate   *vt.* 传播、宣传
sensuous   *a.* 感官上的
dissolved in   溶入
monarchy   *n.* 君主制
prompt   *vt.* 促进、激起
splendor   *n.* 光彩、壮丽
majesty   *n.* 权威、威严
grandeur   *n.* 壮丽、宏伟
aristocracy   *n.* 贵族、贵族统治
pomp   *n.* 浮华、盛况、壮丽
ornate   *a.* 华丽
elaborate   *a.* 精心制作的；复杂的
undertone   *n.* 底色；色调
undulating   *a.* 波状的，波浪起伏的
theatricality   *n.* 戏剧风格
maternally   *adv.* 母性的
transverse   *adj.* 横向的
ravage   *vt.* 破坏；掠夺
sovereign   *n.* 君主
centrifugal   *a.* 离心的
parterre   *n.* 花坛区
grove   *n.* 树丛

Chapter Eleven   The Eighteenth Century

导读

18世纪，众多关于人性和社会的新思想、新观念引发了广泛而激烈的争论，随着科学发现与科学思想的传播，理性主义思潮发展成为一种运动，称为启蒙运动。许多在17世纪还处于纯粹科学研究领域的知识，到了18世纪已经运用于解决实际问题。

随着中产阶级财富的增长，教育程度的提高，社会影响力进一步扩大，对艺术的资助不再局限于宫廷，而是扩展到巴黎的整个上层社会。18世纪初，宫廷生活从凡尔赛回迁巴黎，此时的巴黎城市建设已初具规模，建筑师和艺术家关注的焦点从建筑的外部形象转向内部装饰，从庄严厚重的政治和宗教主题转向优雅轻松的生活趣味，因此，在巴洛克建筑中常常采用洛可可风格的室内装饰。

洛可可是一种装饰艺术风格，是在巴洛克建筑艺术的基础上发展起来的，被视为巴洛克风格的延续，主要表现在室内装饰上，例如，贵族府邸、上流社会聚会的沙龙。洛可可风格的装饰纤巧精致，多用自然题材作曲线，如卷涡波状、卷草舒花、缠绵盘曲，连成一体；色彩娇艳粉嫩，光泽闪烁，象牙白和金黄是其流行色；常用玻璃镜、水晶灯强化效果。

11.1 Socio-economic Background

In Europe, the eighteenth century was a period of intellectual, social, and political development with radical new ideas and discussion. This time is often referred to as the Age of Enlightenment, for it was in the 18th century that the ideas of the previous 100 years were implemented on a broad scale. The scientific discoveries overturned many traditional concepts and introduced new perspectives on nature and man's place within it. It has also been called the Age of Reason. At its core was a critical questioning of traditional institutions, customs, and morals, based on the realistic recognition of the sad state of the human condition and the need for major reforms.

In the eighteenth century the political map of Europe changed as Russia and Prussia became European powers. Meanwhile, the conflict between France and Britain over the commercial interests in India and America resulted in victory for Britain. Britain, replacing France, moved into a dominant position in Europe, acquiring a huge empire. The increase of wealth in Britain was seen as associated with political and commercial freedom

The Enlightenment

The Enlightenment thinkers believed that systematic thinking might be applied to all areas of human activity, in their explorations of the individual, society and the state. They emphasized the equality of all individuals and believed reason held the key to creating an ideal society. The Englishman John Locke wrote that people have certain natural rights like life, liberty and property, and that governments were created in order to protect these rights. The movement helped create the intellectual framework for the American and French Revolutions, and many historians and philosophers credit the Enlightenment with the later rise of classical liberalism, socialism, democracy, and modern capitalism.

The Enlightenment was European-wide, with France and Scotland of particular importance. In France, Enlightenment was based in the salons. A salon is a gathering of people under the roof of an inspiring host, held partly to amuse one another and partly to refine the taste and increase the knowledge of the participants through conversation.

Scots thinker Adam Smith believed that the wealth of a nation came from free trade and manufacture. He held that the state had only three functions: to protect society, to defend people against injustice and to ensure that there was an infrastructure (good roads, canals, harbors, etc.). By the end of the century, Adam Smith's economic ideas would provide the intellectual basis for the development of modern capitalism.

One of the greatest intellectual achievements of the age was the 35 volume *Encyclopedia* or *Classified Dictionary of the Sciences, Arts and Trades* (1751–1772), published in France. This huge project involved hundreds of scholars, writers and men of practical experience to contribute articles and illustrations, providing information and opinion on every conceivable topic.

The new intellectual forces spread to urban centers across Europe, notably England, Scotland, the German states, the Netherlands, Poland, Russia, Italy, Austria, and Spain, then jumped the Atlantic into the European colonies, where it influenced

Benjamin Franklin and Thomas Jefferson, among many others, and played a major role in the American Revolution. The political ideals of the Enlightenment influenced the *American Declaration of Independence, the United States Bill of Rights, the French Declaration of the Rights of Man and of the Citizen.*

In academia, for the first time, science became a central piece of public discourse. Until then, much of scientific inquiry was pursued by a relatively small group of academics whose writings did not enjoy widespread circulation.

Beginning in the late 17th century, there was a major development in academia that would bring about a rapid democratization of scientific knowledge. The first was the foundation of the Paris Academy and the Royal Society of London, two institutions whose primary purpose was to do scientific research and report their conclusions to the public. Over the succeeding decades, several other institutions would be founded on the model of these two, including the Berlin Academy, the St. Petersburg Academy, the Turin Society, and many others.

The second major development in academic life was the rise of scientific journals. These publications were often produced by the academies themselves though a fair number were produced independently. These new journals circulated to a wide audience that included many outside the scientific community. In one sense, these are among the first "popular science" magazines, in that scientific results were reported to an audience of non-specialists.

11.2 Rococo Art and Architecture

By the 18th century, Baroque art was falling out of fashion as many deemed it too melodramatic and also gloomy, and it developed into the Rococo, which emerged in France. The architects and artists of the time turned away from monumental architecture Versailles represented. The intention was for something lighter and more expressive of pleasure.

The Rococo style of art emerged in France in the early 18th century as a continuation of the Baroque style, also referred to as Late Baroque. Rococo art was even more elaborate than the Baroque, but it was less serious and more playful. The artistic movement no longer placed an emphasis on politics and religion, focusing instead on lighter themes such as romance, celebration, and appreciation of nature.

In general, Rococo is mostly an interior style. During the early 18th century, when

136 An Introduction to Western Culture and Art

Fig. 11.1
Musee Carnavalet. It shows the development in Parisian interior design since 17th century.
French Rococo art was at home indoors, metalwork, porcelain figures, furniture and etc.

Fig. 11.2
Catherine Palace, St. Petersburg, Russia, completed in 1756.
Rococo art and architecture made strong usage of creamy, pastel colors, curves and gold.

Fig. 11.3
Ballroom

Fig. 11.4
Dininghall

court life moved back to Paris from Versailles, Paris was already built up and so rather than engaging in major architectural additions, the wealthy and aristocratic simply renovated the interiors of the existing buildings. Therefore, we are more likely to find Rococo interiors in Baroque style buildings.

French Rococo art was at home indoors, metalwork, porcelain figures, furniture and etc. Especially, furniture was lighthearted, physically and visually, and could be easily moved around for gatherings. French upper classes sought to outfit their homes in fashionable style. (Fig. 11.1)

In 1835 the *Dictionary of the French Academy* stated that the word Rococo usually covers the kind of ornament, style and design associated with Louis XV's reign and the beginning of that of Louis XVI. It includes therefore, all types of art produced around the middle of the 18th century in France.

There are some notable differences between Rococo and Baroque architecture. Despite both being richly decorated, they had different themes. The Baroque was more serious, political, placing an emphasis on religion, and was often characterized by Christian themes, like heroic battles or religious figures (as a matter of fact, the Baroque began in Rome as a response to the Protestant Reformation). On the contrary, Rococo was more secular, focused on the carefree aristocratic life and on lighthearted romance.

In contrast to the heavier themes and darker colors of the Baroque, the Rococo was characterized by an opulence, grace, playfulness, and lightness. Rococo motifs include numerous curves and decorations, as well as the usage of pale colors and creamier shades. Furthermore, it sought inspiration from the artistic forms and ornamentation of Far Eastern Asia, such as porcelain figurines. This artistic change became well established, first in the royal palace and then throughout French high society.

Rococo artists opted for a more florid and graceful approach to Baroque art and architecture. Rococo art and architecture in such a way was ornate, florid and made strong usage of creamy, pastel colors, curves and gold. Where Baroque architecture favors symmetry, Rococo favors asymmetry. With regards to interior decoration, Rococo rooms were designed as total works of art with elegant and ornate furniture, small sculptures, ornamental mirrors, and etc. (Fig. 11.2–Fig. 11.6)

138　An Introduction to Western Culture and Art

Fig. 11.5
Interior decoration
Rococo rooms were designed as a total work of art with elegant and ornate furniture, small sculptures, ornamental mirrors, reliefs, and wall paintings.

Fig. 11.6
Furniture was lighthearted, and could be easily moved around for gatherings.

Typical defining characteristics of the Rococo style:
Curved and natural patterns
Asymmetrical design
Ornate, and graceful
Often gilt

New Words and Expressions

academia   *n.* 学术界
public discourse   *n.* 公共话语
democratization   *n.* 民主化
Rococo   *n. & a.* 洛可可风格
deem   *vt.* 认为；断定为
melodramatic   *a.* 过度夸张或戏剧化的
gloomy   *a.* 沉闷或压抑的
opulence   *n.* 富裕；丰富
figurine   *n.* （用陶土、刻石等制成的）小雕像、小塑像
florid   *a.* 绚丽的
pastel   *a.* 清淡柔和的色彩
gilt   *a. & n.* 镀金的

Chapter Twelve   The Nineteenth Century

导读

19世纪后半叶，西欧和美国都进入了资本主义经济的高速发展阶段。工业革命带来技术突飞猛进，特别是新能源与新材料的结合使城市迅速扩张，产生了交通运输、城市规划、人口居住等一系列新问题，城市对大型公共建筑和商业项目的需求剧增：政府大厦、银行大厦、图书馆、博物馆、剧院、学校、厂房、车站、博览会展馆等。一些建筑由于其功能特殊可以采用全新的形式，如厂房、车站、博览会展馆等，而另一些建筑很难在短时期内形成崭新的形式，设计师只能从古典风格中选取合乎其实际需求的形式，这便是在欧美出现的古典复兴运动。

12.1 Socio-economic Background

In the nineteenth century, the political map changed on the Continent and worldwide, with the unification of Germany and Italy, and the collapse of Spain and Portugal, which lost their overseas empires in wars of liberation throughout Central and South America. By the end of the century Germany was the strongest Continental industrial and military power, while Great Britain remained the principal trading country of Europe and the main sea power. After the defeat of the French Empire in the Napoleonic Wars, the British Empire grew rapidly and boasted unchallenged dominance, extending its overseas territories and controlling a fifth of the world's land and one quarter of the world's population. English became the dominant language.

The 19th century was also an era of rapidly accelerating scientific discovery and invention, with significant developments in the fields of mathematics, physics, chemistry, biology, electricity, and metallurgy that laid the foundation for the technological advances of the 20th century. The Industrial Revolution began in Great Britain and spread to continental Europe and North America. This era witnessed the industrialization of northern Europe.

The harnessing of coal and steam energy combined with new mechanized technologies and industrial materials, especially iron, steel and glass, brought sweeping changes throughout the urban settings. The introduction of railroads allowed goods and people to be transported at faster speeds than ever before in history. Soon, large numbers of goods were being produced in factories and many people settled in the cities where the factories were located. These great societal changes fueled major urbanization movements. In addition, advances in medicine and disease prevention accelerated population growth in the western world and the population doubled during the 19th century. Numerous cities surpassed populations of a million during this century. London became the world's largest city and capital of the British Empire.

The economic model of the West also began to change, with mercantilism being replaced by capitalism, in which companies, and later, large corporations, were run by individual investors. Another result was a change in societal hierarchy, where nobility still occupied a high level on the social ladder. Capitalists emerged as a new powerful group, with educated professionals like doctors and lawyers under them, and the various industrial workers at the bottom. These changes were often slow however, with Western society as a whole remaining primarily agricultural for decades.

With the process of industrialization and urbanization, the urban areas were left to the play of economic forces. Building commissions from ecclesiastical, royal and noble patrons were replaced by a new class of public authorities, private patrons and the leaders of modern industrialized state. A changed society required new types of buildings unimagined in a previous age: government offices, banks, hospitals, theaters, libraries, educational institutions, museums, railroad stations, factories, warehouses, commercial buildings such as department stores and a whole range of new types of housing for every social class, from factory workers to industrial barons.

12.2 Architecture and Arts

Two principal characteristics distinguish 19th-century architecture: the use of a variety of historical styles and the development of new materials and structural methods. The first arose from the 19th century architect's perception of continuing the traditional styles of their predecessors. Elements of these earlier styles were put together to give an air of authority to town halls, railway stations, opera houses and legislatures. The second characteristic emerged from the development of new materials as a result of the new industrial needs.

The new situation created by the industrial and social revolutions produced a multitude of new building tasks. The church and the palace lost their importance as leading tasks, the monument, the museum, and dwelling, the theatre, the exhibition hall, the factory and the office building in turn took over their role. All these creations indicated the rise of a new form of life. The monument represented a wish for eternity. The museum was conceived as an "aesthetic church", where all the works of man were brought together, and a manifestation of a new kind of art. The theater revealed human feelings found in their dramatic manifestation. The exhibition, finally, represented the economic values of the new capitalist society.

The new building tasks required innovative engineering and design solutions: the creation of numerous new building styles. However, during the great epochs of the past, certain forms had always been reserved for certain new tasks. The same was the case in the 19th century. New styles of architecture were not created, though the new materials iron and steel were introduced. Designers started to experiment with forms taken from several styles, which represent a cultural heritage or political attitude. One of the ideas was to select for each task the style which suited it best. Churches were usually built in Gothic style, whereas museums and universities were classical. Revivals of past styles occurred and some historical forms were transferred to new types of buildings, the arbitrary use of architectural forms borrowed from the styles of the past.

The truly creative works of this period are the great utilitarian structures of iron and glass, which were used for reasons of cost or as a demonstration of the industrial age. Prefabrication was also invented.

12.2.1 Neoclassicism

Neoclassicism is the name given to Western movements in the decorative and visual arts, literature, theatre, music, and architecture that draw inspiration from the "classical" art and culture of Ancient Greece or Ancient Rome. Neoclassicism was born in Rome in the mid-18th century, but its popularity spread all over Europe, as a generation of European art students finished their Grand Tour (the traditional trip through Italy undertaken by mainly upper-class European young men in search of art, culture and the roots of Western civilization) and returned from Italy to their home countries with newly rediscovered Greco-Roman ideals. The main Neoclassical movement coincided with the 18th-century Age of Enlightenment, and continued into the early 19th century. In architecture, the style continued throughout the 19th, 20th and up to the 21st century.

Neoclassicism in visual arts began in the mid-18th century in opposition to the then-dominant Baroque and Rococo styles. Neoclassical architecture is based on the principles of simplicity and symmetry, which were seen as virtues of the arts of Ancient Greece and Rome, and were more immediately drawn from 16th-century

Chapter Twelve The Nineteenth Century   143

Fig. 12.1
Galleeria Vittorio Emenuele Milan, built in 1865-1877, is Italy's oldest shopping mall. The street is covered by an arching glass and cast iron roof, a popular design for 19th-century large glazed shopping arcades.

Fig. 12.2
Brussels Palace of Justice, 1866-1883. It is reputed to be the largest building constructed in the 19th century.

 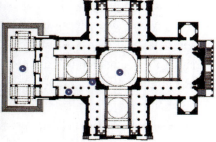

Fig. 12.3
The Pantheon Paris, 1758-1790, an early example of neoclassicism, with a façade modeled on the Pantheon in Rome. The overall design was that of a Greek cross with massive portico of Corinthian columns.

Renaissance Classicism. Neoclassicism was strongest in architecture, sculpture and the decorative arts, where classical models were relatively numerous and accessible. Neoclassicism first gained influence in England and France. (Fig. 12.1–Fig. 12.3)

At the beginning of the 19th century, the city of Paris doubled in population without increasing its space. The majority of Paris was still in medieval style and city center was chaotic, overcrowded, dark, crime-ridden, dangerous and unhealthy.

Meanwhile, France had transitioned between Royal dynasties, Republics, and Empires six different times! Paris was the focal point of revolutionary movements. Napoleon III realized that the narrow streets were easy to barricade and the winding disorganized layout made it difficult for troops to quell rebellions quickly. These unplanned streets were confusing and not efficient for commerce and traffic.

After the decisive defeat of Napoleon at Waterloo in 1815, Paris never recaptured its glory. Inspired by the example of London rebuilt in a massive project after the great fire in 1666, Napoleon III was determined to remake Paris into a great modern capital worthy of the empire.

Napoleon III had a great interest in modern technology, architecture and city planning. He worked closely with Georges-Eugène Haussmann, who initiated the huge project of renovation. One of the most important aspects of the plan was the renovation of Paris's main roads, which brought symmetry to the city. They first concentrated on boulevards, streets, public works (including sewer, water and gas lines), train stations to move large concentrations of people, then architecture. They wanted a well-ordered city, based on a geometric grid with streets running north and south, east and west, having diagonal connections radiating out. Trees were planted to line the boulevards, composing a grand urban landscape. (Fig. 12.4)

While both Napoleon III and Haussmann wanted to modernize Paris, at the same time they were adherents of classical style. They wanted all the buildings to share a unifying classical theme, from the facades of apartment buildings to the construction of major Parisian landmarks. The city was rebuilt with a neoclassical façade that combined elaborate decorative adornments of sculptured friezes, Corinthian columns, Baroque and early Renaissance motifs. Typically five stories, these buildings would feature elaborate balconies. The ground floor would usually be reserved for shops or other businesses. While the outside facade is fancy, Haussmann employed cost saving measures beneath the exterior, and since all the buildings were made in the same style they were able to be built much more cheaply. Such landmarks constructed during this time included the Garnier Opera, Triumphal Arch, and etc. (Fig. 12.5)

Chapter Twelve   The Nineteenth Century   145

Fig. 12.4
Boulevards radiating out from the Triumphal Arch

Fig. 12.5
A neoclassical façade

Fig. 12.6 (left)
The Garnier Opera or
The Opéra de Paris,
1861–1875

Fig. 12.7 (right)
Triumphal Arch,1806–
1836

The Palais Garnier has been referred to as one of the most famous opera houses in the world, a symbol of Paris like Notre Dame Cathedral and the Louvre. This is at least partly due to its use as the setting for a 1910 novel, *The Phantom of the Opera*, especially, the novel's subsequent adaptations in films and Andrew Lloyd Webber's popular 1986 musical. The Triumphal Arch honors those who fought and died for France in the French Revolutionary and the Napoleonic Wars. (Fig. 12.6, Fig. 12.7)

Haussmann essentially remade Paris into what it is today; however, the huge project is not without controversy. There was and still is debate whether the renovation destroyed old Paris or created new Paris. The project destroyed some 20,000 buildings and about 60% of Paris's buildings were rebuilt or transformed. The project was massively over budget.

While there were many negative aspects to the project it did lead to some marked improvements in Paris: disease lessoned, traffic improved, and the quality of life for Parisians improved. Haussmann engineered a new underground sewer system that separated drinking water and waste. His sewer used iron piping and new digging techniques made possible by the Industrial Revolution. The new sewers also provided a source of tourism and became a popular attraction in Paris almost immediately after their completion.

The neoclassical style was international, e.g. the British Museum in London. In America, Neoclassicism was manifested in the Federal style during the Federal Period, when the founding generation consciously chose to associate the nation with the ancient democracies of Greece and the republican values of Rome, such as the White House and the Capitol in Washington, D.C. (Fig. 12.8–Fig. 12.11)

In America, late 18th century architecture and early 19th century building designs were typically based on Roman or Greek architecture—known as "Federal style" or "Greek Revival".

12.2.2 Utilitarian Structures of Iron and Glass

After the middle of the nineteenth century, the large hall (for production and distribution), the office building, and the individual house became the leading tasks which determined the character of urban environment. The hall developed mainly in Europe when iron and glass were adopted for the construction of large exhibition buildings, railway stations, (Fig. 12.14–Fig. 12.16) department stores and factories. Some splendid examples were the Crystal Palace at the first World Exhibition of 1851 in London and the Gallery of Machines at the Paris Universal Exposition of 1889.

Chapter Twelve   The Nineteenth Century   147

Fig. 12.8
The Capitol in Washington, D.C. 1793–1863

Fig. 12.9
The Dome

Fig. 12.10
The British Museum, 1823–1847

Fig. 12.11
Thomas Jefferson's home, 1780–1809.
He designed the house using neoclassical design principles described by Italian Renaissance architect Andrea Palladio.

Fig. 12.12
Crystal Palace at the first World Exhibition of 1851 in London

Fig. 12.13
Pavilion of Machines, Paris Exposition of 1889

Fig. 12.14
The main hall of Musée d'Orsay, originally a railway station built in 1898–1900

Fig. 12.15 (left)
Metal frame construction, Musée d'Orsay

Fig. 12.16 (right)
Gare du Nord 1861–1864, one of the six large terminus railway stations in Paris

The Crystal Palace was a masterpiece of standardization of iron columns, girders and glass panels made with coordinated dimensions and prefabricated in advance. In fact, it was a glass cathedral with the Nave 560 meters long and 137 meters wide, and the arched transept 32 meters high. It was a manifestation of scientific and industrial progress and a new kind of architecture as well. The building gave rise to an era of iron-and-glass construction. (Fig. 12.12)

The Gallery of machines formed a huge glass and metal hall with an area of 115 by 420 meters and a height of 48.324 meters. The main structure consisted of twenty three-winged arches rested on small joints, creating a limitless and luminous space, which may be extended horizontally as well as vertically. (Fig. 12.13)

More spectacular structures of iron, such as the Eiffel Tower and the vast steam-filled railroad stations of Paris and London, demonstrate the engineering marvels of the period and the optimism of a new age. The iron frame construction of the Eiffel Tower, then the tallest structure in the world, captured the imagination of millions of visitors to the 1889 Paris Universal Exposition.

New Word and Expressions

metallurgy   *n.* 冶金
harness   *vt.* 治理；驾驶
utilitarian   *a.* 功利主义的
prefabrication   *n.* （组合房屋的）预制构件
Neoclassicism   *n.* 新古典主义
Grand Tour   *n.* 壮游；文化朝圣
Greco-Roman   *n.* 希腊罗马式的
chaotic   *a.* 混乱的
barricade   *vt.* 设路障
quell   *vt.* 平息；镇压
boulevard   *n.* 林荫大道
diagonal   *a.* 对角线的；斜线的
Garnier Opera   *n.* 加尼叶歌剧院；巴黎歌剧院
Triumphal Arch   *n.* 凯旋门

Chapter Thirteen   The Twentieth Century

导读

现代主义是 20 世纪设计的核心，不但深刻地影响到整个世纪的人类物质文明和生活方式，同时，对本世纪的各种艺术、设计活动（包括工业产品、环境艺术、城市规划）都有决定性的影响。

20 世纪 20 年代到第二次世界大战爆发前后，德国、荷兰、俄国等欧洲国家的建筑师为寻找代表新时代的形式改变设计观念，为在设计中引入民主精神，为大众服务，开始从设计观念、设计风格和形式、建筑材料，建筑方式等各方面进行探索。

13.1 Socio-economic Background

By the late 19th century, the world was dominated by a few great powers, including Britain, the United States, Germany, France, Russia and Austria-Hungary. The years between 1870 and 1914 saw the rise of Germany as the dominant power in Europe. Germany had surpassed Britain to become the world's greatest industrial power. It also had the mightiest army in Europe. France found itself weakened industrially due to its loss of iron and coal mines following the war with Prussia. Britain continued to maintain its vast empire, the largest in world history, though falling behind Germany and the United States in industrial production.

Western inventors and industrialists transformed the West in the late 19th and early 20th centuries. The American Thomas Edison pioneered electricity and motion picture technology. The Wright brothers completed the first successful airplane flight in 1903. The first automobiles were also invented in this period. Petroleum became an important commodity after the discovery it could be used to power machines. Steel was developed in Britain. This very strong metal, combined with the invention of elevators, allowed people to construct very tall buildings, called skyscrapers. In 1876, the first telephone was invented by Alexander Graham Bell. Many became very wealthy from this Second Industrial Revolution, including the American entrepreneurs Andrew Carnegie and John D. Rockefeller.

The Industrial Revolution continued. Influential innovations included steam-powered industrialization, especially the development of railways, and the subsequent advancements in physics, engineering, and architecture associated with it. A major 19th-century engineering achievement was the Crystal Palace, the huge cast-iron and plate glass exhibition hall built for The Great Exhibition of 1851 in London. Glass and iron were used in a similar monumental style in the construction of major railway terminals, and these technological advances led to the building of later structures like the Brooklyn Bridge (1881) and the Eiffel Tower (1889). These engineering marvels radically altered the 19th-century urban environment and people's daily life.

Culturally, the English-speaking nations were in the midst of the Victorian Era, named for Britain's queen. In France, this period is a period of many artistic and cultural achievements. Paris, lit up by gas and electric light, and containing the tallest structure in the world at the time, the Eiffel Tower, was often looked to as an ideal modern city, and served as a model for city planners around the world. Cities grew as never before during this period.

13.2 Architecture and Art

Modern architecture emerged at the end of the 19th century from revolutions in technology, engineering and building materials, and from a desire to break away from historical architectural styles and to invent something that was purely functional and new. The revolution in materials came first, with the use of cast iron, plate glass, and reinforced concrete, to build structures that were stronger, lighter and taller. The Crystal Palace at the Great Exhibition of 1851 was an early example of iron and plate glass construction.

These developments together led to the first steel-framed skyscraper, the ten-story Home Insurance Building in Chicago, built in 1884. This was a response to the shortage of land and high cost of real estate in the center of the fast-growing American cities, and the availability of new technologies, including fireproof steel frames and improvement in the safety elevator, which made tall office and apartment buildings practical. Another important technology for the new architecture was the electric light, which greatly reduced the inherent danger of fires caused by gas in the 19th century.

According to some critics, modernism developed out of the revolt against the effects of the Industrial Revolution and bourgeois values. Some designers believed in the role of art in helping to improve the lives of the urban working classes, in the rapidly expanding industrial cities.

From late 19th century to early 20th century, some art movements emerged attempting to break away from historical styles to designs inspired by function and nature. They were largely a reaction against a perceived decline in standards that were associated with machinery and factory production, or the impoverished state of the decorative arts, like the items displayed in the Great Exhibition of 1851, which were considered to be excessively ornate, artificial and ignorant of the qualities of the materials used.

13.2.1 The Arts and Crafts Movement

The Arts and Crafts movement was an international movement in the decorative and fine arts that began in Britain and flourished in Europe and North America between about 1860s and 1920. It was inspired by the ideas of architect Augustus Pugin, writer John Ruskin, and designer William Morris. It advocated traditional craftsmanship using simple forms, and often medieval, romantic or folk styles of decoration, and its influence continued among craft makers, designers, and town planners long afterwards.

In 1861 Morris, the main inspiration behind the Arts & Crafts Movement, began making furniture and decorative objects commercially, modeling his designs on medieval styles and using bold forms and strong colors. His patterns were based on flora and fauna and his products were inspired by the domestic traditions of the British countryside. In order to display the beauty of the materials and the work of the craftsman, some were deliberately left unfinished, creating a rustic appearance. Truth to materials, structure and function became characteristic of the Arts and Crafts movement.

13.2.2 Art Nouveau

Art Nouveau, which dominated the arts from 1890 to World War I., is an international style of art, including architecture, interior design and most of decorative arts. The architectural style spread from Belgium and France to Germany, Switzerland, Italy, Spain and the rest of Europe, taking on different name and character in each

Chapter Thirteen   The Twentieth Century   153

Fig. 13.1
Guimard designed a series of metro entrances constructed of iron and glass, which could be replicated throughout the system.

Fig. 13.2
Chairs and table with snake motifs 1911

Fig. 13.3
Glassworks 1900

Fig. 13.4
Majolikahaus apartment building Vienna, 1898, modern form decorated with vibrant floral motifs, by Otto Wagner

Fig. 13.5
The glass and steel dome of the department store Galeries Lafayette, Paris, 1912

country. It reached its peak in 1910, and by the beginning of the First World War it was virtually out of fashion. These art movements were replaced first by Art Deco and then by Modernism.

Art Nouveau was a movement to reform design and decoration. It was a reaction against the trend toward industrialization and mechanization. Inspired by natural forms and structures, particularly the curved lines of plants and flowers, and Japanese woodblock printing, Art Nouveau called for renovation of a taste corrupted by mass-produced objects and cluttered urban environments. The buildings were covered with ornament in floral and vegetal forms, which became the most popular signature of Art Nouveau, based on flowers, plants or animals such as butterflies, peacocks, swans and etc. Façades were asymmetrical, and often decorated with colorful ceramic tiles. The decoration usually suggested movement and there was no distinction between the structure and the ornament. (Fig. 13.5)

Art Nouveau was expressed through decoration. In all of these buildings, the architects also designed the furniture and the interior decoration, down to the doorknobs and carpeting. According to the philosophy of the style, art should be a way of life. For many well-off Europeans, it was possible to live in an art nouveau-inspired house with art nouveau furniture, silverware, fabrics, glass and etc. (Fig. 13.2, Fig. 13.3)

Belgium was an early center of the Art Nouveau, thanks largely to the architecture of Victor Horta. The city of Brussels witnessed very strong growth at the turn of the 20th century and this coincided with a beautification program for the city initiated by King Leopold II. When it came to building their houses, the middle-classes, dealers and industrialists chose Art Nouveau as an expression of this new society's modernity and these were designed by three exceptional creators, Victor Horta, Paul Hankar and Henry Van de Velde, amongst many others. (Fig. 13.4)

After the International Exposition in 1889, Paris had shown the world that it was a leader in terms of technological and artistic innovation and had positioned itself at the forefront on the road to the 20th century. Parisians had been complaining of the monotony of the architecture of the boulevards built under Napoleon II by Georges-Eugène Haussmann. They welcomed the colorful and picturesque style of Guimard, who created façades that combined materials and forms that were far removed from preceding architectural styles. As the most renowned Art Nouveau figure in Paris, Guimard was given the commission to design the entrances for the new Paris metro system that is typical of Art Nouveau style. The entrance structures were praised for

Chapter Thirteen   The Twentieth Century   155

Fig. 13.6 (left)
Skeletal organic quality, Casa Batlló

Fig. 13.7 (right)
Staircase, curved lines, scale-like tiles

Fig. 13.8
Interior of the noble floor, the main floor of the building

Fig. 13.9
Undulating stone façade, twisting iron balconies, sculptural elements on the roof, Casa Milà

Fig. 13.10 (left) Entrance

Fig. 13.11 (right) The height of the pillars and ceilings differ; the apartments are arranged around courtyards

their modern and modular design. (Fig. 13.1)

In Spain, a highly original variant of the style, Catalan Modernism, appeared in Barcelona. Its most famous creator was Antoni Gaudi, who used Art Nouveau's floral and organic forms in a very novel way in the Casa Batlló (1904–1906) and Casa Milà (1906–1908), which are most closely related to the stylistic elements of Art Nouveau.

Gaudi conceived architecture as a form of sculpture, with skeletal organic quality. The facade of his buildings has no straight lines. The façade of the Casa Battlo is encrusted with colorful mosaics of stone and ceramic tiles, while the roof is covered in scale-like tiles. The ground floor, in particular, is rather astonishing with tracery, irregular oval windows and flowing sculpted stone work. (Fig. 13.6–Fig. 13.8)

Casa Milà features undulating stone facade, twisting iron balconies and sculptural elements on the roof. The building does not use load-bearing walls, but rests on pillars and arches. With the use of steel the architect is able to create completely irregular floor plans. Even the height of the pillars and ceilings differ from one to another. In order to allow light in all the rooms, the apartments are arranged around two central courtyards, one circular and the other oval shaped. (Fig. 13.9–Fig. 13.11)

However, Art Nouveau was a luxury style, which required expert and highly-paid craftsmen and could not be easily or cheaply mass-produced. One of the few Art Nouveau products that could be mass-produced was the perfume bottle, and these continue to be manufactured in the style today.

13.2.3 Art Deco

Art Deco is a style of visual arts, architecture and design that first appeared in France just before World War I. Art Deco influenced the design of buildings, furniture, jewelry, fashion, cars, movie theatres, trains, ocean liners, and everyday objects.

Art Deco took its name from International Exhibition of Modern Decorative and Industrial Arts held in Paris in 1925. It combined modernist styles with fine craftsmanship and rich materials. The emergence of Art Deco was closely connected with the rise in status of decorative artists, who until late in the 19th century had been considered simply as artisans. The Paris department stores and fashion designers also played an important part in the rise of Art Deco, including the luggage maker Louis Vuitton, silverware firm Christofle, the jewelers Louis Cartier and etc. French designers felt challenged by the increasing exports of less expensive German furnishings, the main purpose of the Exhibit was to promote the French manufacturers of luxury furniture, porcelain, glass, metal work, textiles and other decorative products. The rules of the exhibition required that all work be modern; no historical styles were allowed. To further promote the products, all the major Paris department stores and major designers had their own pavilions.

Art Deco was a pastiche of many different styles, associated with both luxury and modernity. It combined very expensive materials and exquisite craftsmanship put into modernistic forms. From its outset, Art Deco was influenced by the geometric forms of Cubism, the bright colors of Fauvism and stage arts, especially the Ballets Russes，and the exotic styles of China and Japan, India, Persia, ancient Egypt and Maya art. It was also influenced by Streamline, appeared in the 1930s, which featured curving forms and smooth, polished surfaces. The style was used to decorate the first-class salons of ocean liners, deluxe trains, and skyscrapers.

While the Art Deco had a strong influence on luxury product design and art works in France, it had an important impact on architecture and design in the United States in the 1920s and 1930s. The most famous examples were the skyscrapers in New York (as no buildings were permitted in Paris which were higher than Notre Dame Cathedral), including Chrysler Building, the Empire State Building, and Rockefeller Center, which marked the summit of the Art Deco style. It combined modern aesthetics, fine craftsmanship and expensive materials, and became the symbol of luxury and modernity.

The Art Deco architectural style had many features of modernism, including the use of reinforced concrete, glass, steel, chrome, and it rejected traditional historical models, but unlike the modernist style of Le Corbusier and Mies van der Rohe, it made lavish use of decoration and color.

Chrysler Building (completed in 1930) was a giant seventy-seven floor tall

Fig. 13.12
Chrysler Building crowned by a stainless steel spire, having ornate and expensive lobby, designed by William Van Alen.

Fig. 13.13
Miami Beach Art Deco District from 1920s–1930s

advertisement for Chrysler automobiles. Its most striking feature is its pointed, zigzag-detailed crown and spire. The ornamental top was designed with automotive-inspired design. The lobby is decorated with Deco triangles, sharp angles, slightly curved lines, chrome detailing, and a multitude of patterns. (Fig. 13.12)

The Art Deco period saw an enormous increase in travel and tourism, by trains, automobiles, and airplanes, luxury hotels and transport terminals were built in the new style. The city of Miami Beach developed its own particular variant of Art Deco, and became a popular tourist destination in the 1920s and 1930s, particularly attracting visitors from the Northeast United States during the winter. A large number of Art Deco hotels were built, which have been grouped together into an historical area, all about the same height. Most have classic Art Deco characteristics: clear geometric shapes spread out horizontally; streamline features; and often a central tower breaking the horizontal, topped by a spire or dome. A particular Miami Art Deco feature is pastel colors, alternating with white stucco. The neon lighting at night highlights the Art Deco atmosphere. (Fig. 13.13)

The style competed throughout the period with the modernist architecture, and came to an abrupt end in 1939 with the beginning of World War II, and the rise of the strictly functional and unadorned styles of modernism and the International Style of architecture that followed.

13.2.4 Difference and Similarity of the Art Movements

The Arts and Crafts movement took off around the turn of the 20th century, which challenged the tastes of the Victorian era. Inspired by the social reform concerns and the ideals of reformers and designers, it rejected the factory-produced furnishings and decorative accents that prevailed at the time, embracing instead natural beauty and traditional craftsmanship.

Art Nouveau, like the Arts and Crafts, was heavily influenced by nature, but it rejected any historical style while the Arts and Crafts turned to medieval Gothic style. Art Nouveau favored curved lines and organic forms.

Art Deco, emerged after World War I. is characterized by streamlined and geometric shapes. While both the Art Nouveau and Art Deco movements embraced modernist elements, Art Nouveau featured naturalistic but stylized forms often combined with more geometric shapes, particularly arcs, parabolas, and semicircles. Art Deco had many features of modernism, including the use of reinforced concrete, glass, steel, and chrome. It featured bold shapes like sunbursts and zigzags and broad curves.

Fig. 13.14
In the 1860s William Morris established a firm (which became Morris & Co) to design furniture and wallpaper using traditional craftsmanship and centuries-old styles of decoration. Some of his designs are still being produced 150 years later.

Fig. 13.15
Advertising illustrations for bicycle, cigarette and plays, by Alphonse Mucha 1894−1911

Fig. 13.16
Art deco entrance, Chrysler Building

Fig. 13.17
Art Deco Entrance, Rockefeller Center

Fig. 13.18
Cookie Tin in Art Deco style, a combination of floral and geometric pattern, 1914

Main features:

(1) *Arts and Crafts: Popular in the latter half of the 19th century; handcrafted and artisan-made wood, pottery, tile and stained glass; nature motifs done simply; rectilinear forms with stylized decorative motifs of medieval design.* (Fig. 13.14)

(2) *Art nouveau: Popular in the late 19th century; whiplash curves; nature-inspired designs; finely crafted metal and wood.* (Fig. 13.15)

(3) *Art deco: Popular in the 1920s and 1930s; zigzags, sharp angles, curved lines (as in the chair) and stepped designs (as in architecture); mirrors, glass and highly polished metals; influenced by jazz, skyscrapers and cubist art.* (Fig. 13.16-Fig. 13.18)

13.2.5 Modernism

Modernism, in general, includes the activities and creations of those who felt the traditional forms or art, architecture, literature, religious faith, philosophy, social organization, activities of daily life, and even the sciences, were becoming ill-fitted to their tasks and outdated in the new economic, social, and political environment of an emerging fully industrialized world.

In Europe and America, the manufacturing of new building materials, the invention of new construction methods, and the growth of cities inspired architects to experiment with new forms. Chicago architect Louis Sullivan (1856-1924) is often named as the first modern architect, who coined the phrase "form follows function". Le Corbusier thought that buildings should function as "machines for living in", analogous to cars, which he saw as machines for traveling in. Other names that come up are Adolf Loos, Ludwig Mies van der Rohe, and Frank Lloyd Wright, all born in the 19th century. Following this machine aesthetic, modernist designers refused the old styles and structures inherited from Ancient Greece or the Middle Ages. They rejected decorative motifs in design, preferring to emphasize the materials used and pure geometrical forms. These architects presented a new way of thinking about architecture, both structurally and aesthetically. They matched design and modern living, based on the concept that "form follows function". They created geometric and simplified style, without ornament, to express the function of building, as reinforced concrete could be molded into any shape to create enormous spaces without the need of supporting pillars.

Fig. 13.19
The Austrian Postal Savings Bank

Fig. 13.20
Schröder House in Utrecht 1924, an icon of the Modern Movement in architecture

Fig. 13.21
The German Pavilion for the 1929 International Exposition in Barcelona, and the Barcelona chair, Mies van der Rohe

Fig. 13.22
Red and Blue Chair, designed by Gerrit Rietveld, version without colors 1919, version with colors 1923

Fig. 13.23
Free Rocking Chair, 1927

Fig. 13.24 (top)
Cubist Tableware, 1935

Fig. 13.25 (bottom)
Table setting 1931

The Austrian Postal Savings Bank (1904–1906) designed by Wagner demonstrated his intention to express the function of the building, applying the idea of using the construction material itself as a decorative element. The interior was purely functional with a large open space of steel, glass and concrete where the only decoration was the structure itself. (Fig. 13.19)

The German Pavilion for the 1929 International Exposition in Barcelona, known for its simple form and spectacular use of extravagant materials such as marble, is one of best-known landmarks of modernist architecture. It is a work of minimalism (the idea of "less is more"), with glass and concrete walls and clean, horizontal lines. The same features of minimalism can be applied to furniture design, such as the iconic Barcelona chair in the pavilion. (Fig. 13.21)

In Germany, a modernist industrial movement, Deutscher Werkbund (German Work Federation), was created in Munich in 1907. It was a German association of artists, architects, designers, and industrialists, with its goal to bring together designers and industrialists to turn out well-designed, high quality products, and in the process to invent a new type of architecture. The Werkbund became an important element in the development of modern architecture and industrial design, particularly in the later creation of the Bauhaus school of design, improving the competitiveness of German companies in global markets, by means of education, organizing exhibitions and publishing the problems and themes of designs. Bauhaus simply became synonymous with modern design. (Fig. 13.20, Fig. 13.22–Fig. 13.26)

Bauhaus was a German art school operational from 1919 to 1933 that sought a new integration of art and technology. To rebuild the country after Germany's defeat in World War I, Bauhaus created a new "rational" social housing in radically simplified forms that are functional, without ornamentation of any kind, and on the budget. Generally, Bauhaus buildings have flat roofs, smooth façades, and cubic shapes. Colors are white, gray, or black. Floor plans are open and furniture is functional. Popular construction methods of the time—steel-frame with glass curtain walls—were used for both residential and commercial architecture.

At the same time in the US, Frank Lloyd Wright set out to break all the traditional rules and created his famous Prairie Houses. He was designing the house with straight lines, flat roofs and plenty of light. The emphasis was laid on open plans, simple geometry and horizontal lines, encouraging the family to gather and establishing an integration of interior and exterior environment. His design set a new style for suburban living. (Fig. 13.27, Fig. 13.28)

Bauhaus style spread to the United States and developed into the International Style, with an emphasis more on architectural style, form and aesthetics than the social aspects of the modern movement as emphasized in Europe. American International style buildings tend to be geometric, monolithic skyscrapers with these typical features: a rectangular solid with six sides (including ground floor) and a flat roof; a curtain wall completely of glass; no ornamentation; and stone, steel, glass construction materials. One of the most famous examples of the International Style is the United Nations Headquarters in NYC completed in 1952. While German Bauhaus architecture had been concerned with the social aspects of design, America's International Style became a symbolism of Capitalism. It is the favored architecture for office buildings and is also found in upscale homes built for the rich. (Fig. 13.29, Fig. 13.30)

Modernism first emerged in the early twentieth century, and by the 1920s, the prominent figures of the movement—Le Corbusier, Walter Gropius, and Ludwig Mies van der Rohe—had established their reputations. The pioneers of the movement had strong ambition and sense of social responsibility that architecture should raise the living conditions of the masses. They were striving for "honest" approaches to building design that focused on functional efficiency. They held a firm belief that in creating a better architecture, a better world would ultimately follow.

The key features in modernist design included function, progress, anti-historicism and social morality. However it was not until after the Second World War that it gained mass popularity, after modernist planning was implemented as a solution to address social problems of this decade, such as slum clearance and providing better housing for urban populations living in poverty. Many modernist projects were initially successful, and the public came to associate this aesthetic with prosperity and progress. There is no doubt that this new architecture would improve towns and the living situation. But the movement could not adequately comprehend and cater for the social dynamics of family and communities, and some of their efforts were accused of inhumane planning process that did not properly consider those who were to live in the planned developments, and some modernist aesthetic was considered to be dull. As a result, many modernist buildings were pulled down in the seventies.

Common themes of modern architecture include:
（1）*Simplicity and clarity of forms and elimination of "unnecessary detail".*
（2）*Visual expression of structure (as opposed to the hiding of structural elements).*

Chapter Thirteen The Twentieth Century 165

Fig. 13.26
Werkbund Housing Estate, Weissenhof, Studttgart 1927

Fig. 13.27
James and Dolores Edwards Residence, Okemos, Michigan, 1949

Fig. 13.28
Goetsch-Winkler House, Okemos, Michigan, 1940

Fig. 13.29
International style, Chicago

Fig. 13.30
International style, Paris

（3）*The concept of "truth to materials", meaning that the true nature or natural appearance of a material ought to be seen rather than concealed or altered to represent something else.*
（4）*Use of industrially-produced materials; adoption of the machine aesthetic.*
（5）*Particularly in International Style modernism, a visual emphasis on horizontal and vertical lines.*

New Words and Expressions

cast-iron   *adj.* 铸铁的；坚固的
plate glass   *n.* 平板玻璃
reinforced concrete   *n.* 钢筋混凝土
revolt   *n.* 反感；反抗
impoverish   *vt.* 使贫穷；使枯竭
Arts and Crafts Movement   *n.* 工艺美术运动
Art Nouveau   *n.* 新艺术运动
Art Deco   *n.* 装饰艺术
woodblock printing   *n.* 版画；木刻版印刷术
renovation   *n.* 革新；修复；翻新

clutter vt. 使凌乱；胡乱地填满
ceramic tile n. 瓷砖；陶瓷砖
coincide vi. 同时发生；巧合
monotony n. 单调；千篇一律
Catalan adj. 加泰罗尼亚的；加泰罗尼亚语的
encrust with vt. 镶嵌
scale-like 鳞片状
tracery n. 窗饰；花饰窗格（In architecture, tracery is the stonework elements that support the glass in a Gothic window）
undulating a. 波浪起伏的
load-bearing wall n. 沉重墙
pastiche n. 拼凑的艺术作品；合成的作品；集锦
modernistic a. 现代派的；现代主义的
Cubism n. 立体派；立体主义
Fauvism n. 野兽派（画派）
Ballets Russes 俄罗斯芭蕾舞团
streamline n. 流线型
deluxe a. 高级的；奢华的
Notre Dame Cathedral 巴黎圣母院
chrome n. 铬
lavish a. 过分慷慨的；非常浪费的；无节制的
zigzag n. & adj. 之字形；Z字形；锯齿形的；之字形的；曲折的
variant n. & adj. 变体；转化；不同的；多样的
pastel a. & n. 柔和的；粉蜡笔的；粉蜡笔；粉蜡笔画
stucco n. 灰泥
parabola n. 抛物线
rectilinear a. 直线运动的；形成直线的
whiplash n. 鞭打
extravagant adj. 奢侈的；放纵的
minimalism n. 极简主义；简约主义
Deutscher Werkbund 德意志制造联盟；德意志工作联盟
Bauhaus 包豪斯建筑学派；包豪斯风格
synonymous a. 同义的；同义词的
monolithic a. 巨石的；庞大的

References

1. 叶胜年，巫德安．欧洲历史名人 [M]．上海：上海外语教育出版社，2002．
2. [英] 西德韦尔．欧洲文化概况 [M]．北京：外语教学与研究出版社，2008．
3. [美] 威廉·弗莱明，玛丽·马里安．艺术与观念 [M]．宋协立，译．北京：北京大学出版社，2008．
4. 史建．大地之灵 [M]．济南：山东画报出版社，1998．
5. 王受之．世界现代建筑史 [M]．北京：中国建筑工业出版社，1999．
6. 常俊跃，黄洁芳，赵永青．欧洲文化入门 [M]．北京：北京大学出版社，2011．
7. 彭家海．西方文化引论 [M]．武汉：华中师范大学出版社，2009．
8. 叶胜年．西方文化史鉴 [M]．上海：上海外语教育出版社，2002．
9. Christian Norberg-Schultz. *Meaning in Western Architecture* [M]. Milano: Electa Spa, 1974.
10. Stephen J. Campbell，Michael W. Cole. *A New History of Italian Renaissance Art* [M]. London: Thames & Hudson, 2012.
11. Hugh Honour & John Fleming. *A World History of Art* [M]. London: Laurence King Publishing, 2009.
12. Gina Pischel，*A World History of Art* [M]. New York: Golden Press, 1968.
13. Cecil Stewart. *Gothic Architecture (Simpson's History of Architectural Development Vol.III)* [M]. London: Longmans, Green and Co LTD，1961.
14. Robin Doak. *Great Empire of the Past: Empire of the Islamic World* [M]. Santa Barbara, California: Shoreline Publishing Group LLC, www.factsonfile.com.
15. David Watkin. *A History of Western Architecture* [M]. London: Laurence King Publishing, 2011.
16. Markus Hattstein. *Islam Art and Architecture* [M]. Reisen: Potsdam: H.F. Ullmann, 2010.
17. Victoria Charles, Klaus H. Carl. *Romanesque Art* [M]. New York: Parkstone Press, 2008.

18. Ancient Egypt, Wikipedia, the free encyclopedia Ancient Greece—history, mythology, art, war, culture, society...www.ancientgreece.com.
19. Ancient Roman Culture, http.//www.mnsu.edu.
20. Culture of Ancient Rome, Wikipedia.org.
21. Western Culture, Wikipedia, the free encyclopedia.
22. History of Western Civilization, Wikipedia, the free encyclopedia.
23. Middle Ages, Wikipedia, the free encyclopedia.
24. Medieval art, Wikipedia, the free encyclopedia.
25. Towns in the Middle Ages, http://history-world.org/midtowns.htm.
26. Church of Holy Sepulchre, http://biblewalks.com/Sites/Sepulcher.html.
27. Romanesque Art, http://en.wikipedia.org/wiki/Romanesque_art.
28. Italian Renaissance Wikipedia, the free encyclopedia.
29. Renaissance architecture, Wikipedia, the free encyclopedia.
30. Essential World Architecture Images, www. essential- architecture.com.
31. Age of Enlightenment, Wikipedia, the free encyclopedia.
32. The Rococo Style, the Architectureist, Nov. 8, 2012.
33. Rococo, Wikipedia, the free encyclopedia.
34. Early Christian art and architecture, Wikipedia, the free encyclopedia.
35. The Cultural Studies Reader, Simon During, Routledge, 1999.
36. Art, Design and Visual Thinking, http://www.char.txa.cornell.edu/art/decart/artcraft/artcraft.htm.
37. Art Nouveau European Route., http://coupdefouet.eu/en/cities.php Jun. 2015.
38. Baron Haussmann and the modernization of Paris, http://www.museumofthecity.org/project/haussmann-and-revival-of-paris/.
39. Early Applications of Linear Perspective, https://www.khanacademy.org/humanities/renaissance-reformation/early- renaissance1/beginners-renaissance-florence/a/early-applications-of-linear-perspective.
40. Arts and Crafts Movement, http://www.visual-arts-cork.com/history-of-art/arts-and-crafts.htm.

致 谢

感谢西安建筑科技大学艺术学院博士生导师杨豪中教授、长安大学孙家驹教授、密西根州立大学亚洲研究专业馆员吴宪博士在本书的编写过程中给予的帮助和支持。

感谢我的亲人、朋友和同事鼎力相助，使这本教材中各种艺术风格的图片资料更加丰富充实，笔者在此一并表示感谢。

1. 霍秦：图 1.7；1.8；1.13；1.14；7.1
2. 马振东：图 5.7-5.10
3. 冯怡平：图 5.12
4. 李燕：图 5.13；11.3；11.7
5. 张勤：图 7.4
6. 叶三：图 8.14
7. 黄旭梅：图 10.6-10.7
8. 戴红：图 10.9
9. 赵友斌：图 11.4-11.6
10. 马至融：图 11.2
11. 杨阳：图 12.9
12. 冯贻良：图 12.11
13. 王钢：图 13.12；13.16
14. 图 2.2 https://www.ancient.eu/image/4518/
15. 图 5.3-5.5 St. Peter's Basilica
    https://images.search.yahoo.com/search/images;
16. 图 5-16 The organization of some mature Romanesque churches
    https://images.search.yahoo.com/search/images;
17. 图 6.9 The Great Mosque in Cordoba
    https://images.search.yahoo.com/search/images?p=Cordoba%2C+the+Great+Mosque
18. 图 7.6 Hagia Sophia
    https://images.search.yahoo.com/search/images;
19. 图 9.20 The Tempietto
    https://upload.wikimedia.org/wikipedia/commons/1/18/Tempietto_del_Bramante_Roma_HDR_2013_03.jpg
20. 图 12.10 Crystal Palace at the first World Exhibition of 1851
    https://en.wikipedia.org/wiki/The_Great_Exhibition
21. 图 12.11 Pavilion of Machines, Paris Exposition of 1889
    https://commons.wikimedia.org/wiki/File:CLC_528_-_PARIS_-_Galerie_des_Machines.JPG